Seeing
God
in the
Ordinary

Seeing God in the Ordinary

A Theology of the Everyday

Michael Frost

HENDRICKSON
PUBLISHERS

Hendrickson Publishers, Inc.
P.O. Box 3473
Peabody, Massachusetts 01961-3473

Printed in the United States of America
ISBN 1-56563-514-0
Second printing — March 2005

Seeing God in the Ordinary: A Theology of the Everyday is re-
vised from *Eyes Wide Open: Seeing God in the Ordinary* and is
published under agreement between Hendrickson Publishers, Inc., and Albatross Books Pty. Ltd.

First published in Australia, 1998
Albatross Books Pty. Ltd.
P.O. Box 320, Sutherland
NSW 2232, Australia

Library of Congress Cataloging-in-Publication Data

Frost, Michael, 1961–
     Seeing God in the ordinary: a theology of the
  everyday   /   Michael Frost.
         p. cm.
     Includes bibliographical references.
     ISBN 1-56563-514-0 (pbk.)
     1. Christian life.   2. Imagination—Religious aspects—
Christianity.   I. Frost, Michael, 1961—Eyes wide open.
II. Title
BV4501.2 .F7675 2000
230—dc21

00-026780

This book is dedicated to my daughters
Courtney, Kendall, and Fielding:
six of the widest eyes I've ever seen.

Contents

Lord, you have searched me and you know all about me. When I sit down or when I get up, you know about it. You know my thoughts before I have them. You check the road before me; you're acquainted with all my ways.

You know my next sentence before it's reached my tongue. You're in front of me, behind me, all around me, and you lay your hand on me. It's almost too much to take in—I can barely grasp it.

Psalm 139

To God above, we dedicate our song;
to leave him unadored, we never dare.
For he is present in each busy throng;
in every solemn gathering, he is there.
The sea is his, and his each crowded port.
In every place, our need of him we feel;
for we his offspring are.

Aratus of Soli
The Phaenomena

Georges Bernanos' classic French novel, *The Diary of a Country Priest*, ends with the painful death from stomach cancer of the decent young curate—the country priest of the title. Through his difficult life, as recounted for us in his journal, he appears as a beacon in a dark and dangerous world. The church into which he felt called is beset by corruption and deceit. Bernanos, a devoted Christian and fiercely patriotic Frenchman, presents the good and honest young priest as a foil to the excesses of the church of his day. The other priests are self-absorbed and seriously flawed, and Christ's reputation suffers at their hands.

As he lies dying, we are forced to wonder at the harshness of his struggle. He can no longer keep his diary. Another priest has been called to perform the last rites, but has not yet arrived. We discover the fate—and the wisdom—of the curate through a letter written by the friend who was with him at the very end:

> "The priest was still on his way, and finally I was bound to voice my regret that such delay threatened to deprive my comrade of the final consolations of our church. He did not seem to hear me. But a few moments later,

he put his hand over mine and his eyes entreated me to draw closer to him. He then uttered these words almost in my ear. And I am quite sure I have recorded them accurately, for his voice, though halting, was strangely distinct.

'Does it matter? Grace is everywhere . . .'

I think he died just then."

Introduction

THIS IS ESSENTIALLY MY VERY HUMBLE AT-tempt at a theology of the ordinary, bearing in mind that nothing is ever as ordinary as it seems. I guess I'm concerned that in my travels, I see a growing interest in what God is doing and how God is revealing himself and his will that is always couched in spectacular terms. It's as if we think God can operate only through dramatic displays of supernatural power.

In many respects, I feel as though all these preachers and church leaders who are calling for us to stop limiting God and wake up and see God doing "a new thing" are in fact limiting God themselves—to the extraordinary.

Well, I certainly don't want to be the one to rule God out of the extraordinary. The Bible and the history of the church are filled with examples of spectacular visitations of God's Spirit. But I'm also keen for us to be able to see him visiting us in the most simple and ordinary, and yet transformative, ways.

One of my students recently gave me a Zen poem given to him by his Buddhist brother. It is filled with wisdom and reminds us of a spirituality that, I believe, is in keeping with the affirmations of the Bible. It begins:

> How I long for supernatural powers!
> Said the novice mournfully to the holy one.
> I see a dead child
> and I long to say, *Arise!*
> I see a sick man
> I want to say, *Be healed!*
> I see a bent old woman
> I long to say, *Walk straight!*
> Alas, I feel like a dead stick in paradise.
> Master, can you confer on me
> supernatural powers?

The hunger for spectacular supernatural power is a typical one for many of us. We yearn for an experience of the holy that transcends death, sickness, and human frailty. There seems to be a lot of calling out these days, "Master, can you confer on me supernatural powers?" But the poem continues:

The holy one shook his head fretfully;
How long have I been with you
and you know nothing?
How long have you known me
and learned nothing?
Listen, I have walked the earth for eighty years:
I have never raised a dead child,
I have never healed a sick man,
I have never straightened an old woman's spine.

> Children die,
> men grow sick, the aged fall
> under a stigma of frost.

The holy one goes on to berate his student's ravenous hunger for supernatural powers. He tells him that not only does he, the holy one, have no such powers, but that his student certainly cannot be trusted with them. Far better, he says, to perfect natural powers than crave supernatural ones. By natural powers, he means discipline and righteousness: "to see and not be seduced/to hear and not be deafened/to taste and not be eaten/to touch and not be huckstered." These are truly miraculous things, he says.

He concludes:

> Do you seek miracles?
> Listen—go
> draw water, hew wood
> break stones—
> how miraculous!

Blessed is the one
who walks this earth
five years, fifty years, eighty years
and deceives no one and curses no one
and kills no one.

As Christians we have a clear vision that no one can perfect natural powers and live a blameless life. For this reason, Christ has died—to set us free from the consequences of our fallenness. This is truly miraculous! But the point of the poem is not lost on me. It condemns those who would look to the heavens for the extraordinary, when such so-called ordinary things as drawing water from a river or building a wooden chair can be demonstrations of wonder. It condemns those who think the miraculous is accompanied only by celestial bells and whistles, when to live life embracing fidelity and honesty is a miracle in itself these days.

Incidentally, the great G. K. Chesterton once contrasted how Christian saints are depicted in art as opposed to how Buddhist saints are depicted: ". . . perhaps the shortest statement of it is that the Buddhist saint always has his eyes shut, while the Christian saint always has them wide open. The Buddhist saint has a sleek and harmonious body, but his eyes are heavy and sealed with sleep. The medieval saint's body is wasted to its crazy bones, but his eyes are frightfully alive. The Buddhist is looking with a peculiar intentness inwards. The Christian is staring with frantic intentness outwards." Though not so these days, it seems.

I do believe in the supernatural and its power. But I wonder whether we're missing out on too much in pursuing only such expressions of the divine. Our eyes are not so frightfully alive any more. Is God not to be seen in Vincent Van Gogh's *Sunflowers?* Is God not to be seen in the crashing sea? Is God not to be seen in the innocence of a newborn baby's eyes? Or in a rosebud or a character in a film or a book, in a song or in the change of seasons? Can't we hear God in the expressions of love of our friends? Or taste God in good food and conversation?

God's kingdom is extending itself throughout our world. Let's open our eyes to the so-called mundane expressions of God's grace as much as to the spectacular. You'll find them just as breathtaking.

Michael Frost
Sydney, Australia
1999

Chapter 1

A Truth Greatly Reduced

IN 1989, DURING THE LYMAN BEECHER LEC-
tures at Yale University, the biblical scholar
Walter Brueggemann spoke of the church's
mandate to create what he called "poetry in a prose-
flattened world." He rightly asserted that Christians have become so overly concerned with the
technical questions of getting the truth right that we
have squeezed all the *life* out of the gospel:

> The gospel is . . . a truth widely held, but a
> truth greatly reduced. It is a truth that has
> been flattened, trivialized and rendered inane.
> Partly, the gospel is simply an old habit among
> us, neither valued nor questioned. But more
> than that, our technical way of thinking re-
> duces mystery to problem, transforms assur-

ance into certitude, quality into quantity, and so takes the categories of biblical faith and represents them in manageable shapes.[1]

This prose-flattened world of which Brueggemann speaks is a place where language is used to deaden human relationships by tightly defining everything so as to leave others no room to move. Think of an argument where one person continually attacks with, "But you said . . ."; where everything is quoted back to harm the other or to defend one's case. A prose-flattened world has no grace, no allowances for nuance or circumstance. It is clinical, technical, and controlling. It is a world where particulars rule over movement and freedom. Brueggemann's point is that the church must be the *space for grace,* for making allowances, for using language to surprise, to inspire, to relieve, rather than to batter and compete.

We have thought of the gospel as a fragile and precious object. We have held it too tightly, and it has become shapeless and uninteresting. As he said, "There is no danger, no energy, no possibility, no opening for newness."[2]

Much of what passes for the gospel these days is not dramatic or artistic. It is bound by the reason of technique and overly concerned with concreteness. It seems stilted and mechanical. We hear it presented to us week in and week out and, by virtue of the very fact that we *are* believers, we put up with it. It is, indeed, a truth greatly reduced, and it calls forth from us at best a faith greatly reduced, also.

By reducing the gospel to technical, manageable terms, we find ourselves in a time when, in the quest for mystery and spirituality, the typical seeker is gleefully bypassing the church and searching for enlightenment elsewhere. Brueggemann claims that now more than ever the issue of this greatly reduced truth of the gospel requires us to be "poets that speak against a prose world." By prose, he is referring to "a world that is organized in settled formulas, so that even pastoral prayers and love letters sound like memos." By poetry, he asks for much, much more than the standard tract-style equations so common these days:

> By poetry, I do not mean rhyme, rhythm, or meter, but language that moves like Bob Gibson's fast ball, that jumps at the right moment, that breaks open old worlds with surprise, abrasion, and pace. Poetic speech is the only proclamation worth doing in a situation of reductionism.[3]

Now, you don't need to know who Bob Gibson is or what his fast ball looks like to get the impression. Maybe, it's like a Deion Sanders sidestep or a Michael Jordan drive: explosive, unexpected, unrestrained. We have been living in a period where the truth has been greatly reduced to simple formulas. But it's time for a change.

Unfortunately, the best we get in terms of a change these days in the pulpit is the current shift from the old, largely irrelevant formulas to new, glossy, *very* relevant formulas. Rather than a simplistic exposition on the Trinity, now we are likely to get equally simplistic pieces of advice on parenting, marriage enrichment, or "successful" living. Brueggemann concludes that poetic speech is "not moral instruction or problem solving or doctrinal clarification. It is not good advice, nor is it romantic caressing, nor is it a soothing good humor."[4] Poetic preaching will be scary, inviting journeying and discovery on the part of the listener.

Just as poetic speech must be dangerous and exciting, so ought poetic Christian faith. Too much of what passes for Christianity these days minimizes the struggles of real life and appears like a wafer-thin covering, papering over the inconsistencies and uncertainties that confront us regularly.

Our struggle in the twenty-first century will be the struggle to maintain our commitment to the teachings of Jesus and the revelation of the gospel in the New Testament, while endeavoring to rediscover a robust poetic faith that abandons certitude and inanity.

Try-hard spirituality

One of the major contributing factors in the flattening of the gospel's truth has been the false and clearly simplistic distinction many of us make between the so-called religious and nonreligious categories in our lives. We have been seduced into believing that there are certain of our experiences that can justifiably be called sacred, and others that are not. These other experiences have been considered profane or irreligious. At best, they are neutral on the religious scale. At worst, they are depraved and evil.

Therefore, church attendance, prayer, Bible-reading, spiritual reflection, and so on are consigned to the sacred category. Here, we believe, God operates and interacts with us and our experience. On the other hand, attending football games, sunbathing, driving to work, and watching films are profane activities. They aren't considered evil or vile activities. They're just neutral experiences, potentially either good or bad depending on our approach to them. Depending on our personal sensibilities, perhaps watching the "wrong" films, sunbathing topless, or listening to the "wrong" radio station in the car will tip the balance! Invariably, our view seems to be that if they're going to fall one way or the other, they'll likely go downhill.

By separating out our experiences this way and assigning spiritual values to them, we have inadvertently flattened out the truth of the gospel and, I believe, lost much of the potency of the faith of Jesus, who seemed to shatter such distinctions. The dreary, utilitarian prose world wants to classify and label things, making the categories concrete, closed-ended, and manageable. Jesus seemed (almost effortlessly) to be able to eschew this way of seeing life and bring a delightful and poetic spirituality that invaded all of life, answering fewer questions than we might like and reclaiming adventure and uncertainty as important aspects of human experience.

What we end up with when we fall into developing such mechanical equations is a "try-hard" spirituality, an approach to our religious faith that takes such excessive and pathetic levels of effort that it never seems real or natural.

Try-hard is a typically cutting Australian term of disparagement. Usually used as a noun, a try-hard is someone who obviously requires too much effort to be what he or she is claiming to be. For a try-hard, things aren't effortless or natural. They're forced and cloying. Put simply, these people are just trying far too hard. We Christians have been try-hards too long. We should desire an effortless spirituality.

This is not the same as an easy or lazy approach. We know the best things in life involve hard work and sacrifice and that Jesus himself expected this of his followers. But surely the Christian life ought to be a more natural, less forced way of living than it is for many of us. Let me explain what I mean.

There used to be a time in the life of the church in Australia when Protestants in particular had fallen heavily for a fundamentalist version of Christianity that clearly separated the sacred and the profane in the way I described earlier. This separation was clear and enforced with vigor and retribution. Adherents were not permitted to see movies, go to dances, wear makeup, buy newspapers on Sunday, listen to popular music. Church attendance, Bible schools, sacred music, prayer meetings, and so on were the things of God. Football games on the sabbath, bikinis, rock and roll, and Marlon Brando were certainly not.

On the face of it, the church appears largely to have abandoned such formulas these days—until you look more closely. What we have done, in fact, is simply water down this model with a more palatable version of the same thing.

Theologian H. Richard Niebuhr[5] referred to the fundamentalist model as "Christ-against-culture"—for obvious reasons. Anything culturally popular was deemed as evil by the faith community and therefore rejected. But what many Christians do today is not markedly different from the surrounding culture. Niebuhr called this position "Christ-above-culture."

This version of Christianity doesn't so much set the sacred things over and against the profane things in the combative way that fundamentalism does. Rather, it maintains the distinction by placing one *over and above* the other. The "Christ-above-culture" model asserts that we live in a profane world—a place filled with the ordinary, irreligious drudgery of human experience. This world is two-dimensional and unrewarding—until such time as the sacred can be brought to bear on it. In other words, going to work, eating, sleeping, sport, leisure, literature, art, lawn-mowing, car-washing, and picking the kids up from school are religiously neutral experiences. The sacred exists above these things, and those of us who are Christians are to reach up, as it were, and call down the anointing or the blessing. Put another way, these ordinary things of life are of no concern to God until such time as we invite God's blessing upon them.

We speak and act on this understanding so naturally that many of us have never seriously considered what we mean by it. We function as if there is a distant God separated from our evil world who is unable (or unprepared) to draw into our experience until we invite God to do so. Our spiritual life (which we speak of as a component of our experience distinct from everything else) involves us in a quest to be ever calling the sacred down into the ordinariness of this world. We pray for God to be with us in our job interview as if God wouldn't otherwise show up. We invite God into our church meetings as we would an honored guest arriving fashionably late. We pray for blessing on our plans and our dreams as if God hasn't been involved in such planning or dreaming all along.

Such a view flattens the power of the gospel message. It becomes a grid for determining where and when God is at work in our world. It appears like a form guide that gives us the lowdown on "what God thinks" and "how God feels" at any certain time, given any set of circumstances. And all this does is suck the juice out of Christian truth and discard it as an empty shell.

If the poetry of Jesus' message has anything to commend it, it's that God has once and for all drawn near and will never again retreat from this world that God created and loves so dearly. Last Christmas, I spoke at a nativity service in a church in Sydney's western suburbs. It was a dusty hall, and we perched on precarious folding metal chairs. Children enacted the Christmas story and a ventriloquist worked his magic. Then at one point in the meeting a young woman with a huge voice arrived on stage and started belting out the Bette Midler song, "From a Distance." You know how it goes: "God is watching us from a distance." I think it means something like all the world's problems don't look so bad if you move back far enough from them.

It seemed a funny song for a Christmas service, but we all politely listened, until halfway through a woman in the front row could stand it no longer, jumped to her feet, and strode onto the platform, whereupon she burst into singing the same tune but with the following words, "God came near to us, God came near to us, God came near to us, at Christmas." Both women entered into a duel of sorts, each trying to outdo the other with her voice and her version of the lyrics.

It soon became obvious that this had been planned, and it communicated a very effective message. You see, while we function at one level in the belief that God came near at Christmas when God chose to inhabit the human experience, we often live our lives as if God is really just watching us from a distance. In our daily experience both sets of lyrics might be ringing in our ears, but it's fairly obvious which one is being sung the louder.

When you spend a good deal of your existence either functioning as if God isn't interested or desperately trying to work out the formula to get God interested, you're likely to remain trapped in what has been called exhausted coping. Our try-hard spirituality never seems the antidote to such exhaustion.

Not that we Christians are alone in this. Many people who search their horoscopes for an experience of the sacred in the midst of the profane can be as try-hards as many of us, as can those who "use" crystals for empowerment or those who attend workshops to unlock their sacred intuitive forces within them. Wherever there is a forced, neurotic, cloying desperation to haul "otherness" into the now, you can bet you're dealing with try-hard spirituality. And it always runs out of steam eventually, because we humans simply don't have enough energy to sustain it.

Try-hards live in a prose-flattened world. This is a world that operates under strict contracts and unyielding policies. It claims, "If you do this, I will do that." Tryhards need such certainty. They need simple equations to govern their lives. But the faith of the Christians, as of the Hebrews before them, is a faith based on a covenant, not a contract. It is based in a fluid, dynamic personal relationship with God, not just on a legal procedure filled with technicalities. Jesus was a poet who came to set us free from these inadequate formulas. In 1994, I published my first book, *Jesus the Fool*,[6] in which I attempted to capture something of this notion. Jesus, like the medieval jester, so undermined the mechanical and technical prose of his world that his songs, his wit, and his poetry turned the world upside down. The number of people who were offended by the idea of calling Jesus a fool surprised me. Even those who read the book and saw the point were unable to be comfortable with it. I fear we may have concretized language and constricted ideas so much that we're stuck in the old formulas.

Jesus' radical line on truth was that God, fed up with the gulf that existed between God and God's world, drew near at last. The incarnation, the doctrine of God in human form (as difficult as it is to understand), has sustained Jesus' followers ever since. Our God is *here;* our God has entered into our experience. Faith is all it takes. The faith to risk living as if it's true. The "Christ-above-culture" framework undermines the idea of the incarnation. It strips it of its meaning and sends God back to heaven, far away, awaiting our intermittent invitations. If Jesus is worth following, it's because he is God and shows us how to live in an effortless realization that the kingdom is to be experienced all around us and all the time.

The kingdom is at hand

The kingdom of God is a tricky idea, but no one doubts that it is in fact the central theme of the teaching and preaching of Jesus. In its most abstract sense, the kingdom is the rule of God and the realm of God's blessings, and the New Testament affirms clearly that the kingly rule of God has broken into history in the life of Jesus; it has brought to people the blessings of God's reign. In Jesus' Parable of the Leaven in Matthew 13:33, the kingdom of God is viewed as a present reality, here and now. It's like leaven, spreading gradually but surely throughout the whole. Theologian Millard Erickson puts it this way: its growth will be extensive (it will spread throughout the entire world) and intensive (it will become dominant).[7]

The kingdom is not something removed and far from our experience. In Luke 10 Jesus says to his disciples, "Whenever you enter a town and they receive you, eat what is set before you; heal the sick in it and say to them, *'The kingdom of God has come near to you.'*"[8]

In the models by H. Richard Niebuhr mentioned earlier, the kingdom of God exists in the sacred category, separated from the rest of human experience. But in Jesus' conception of things, the kingdom is not separated at all. The wheat and the

weeds grow together as far as he was concerned.
Any separation would be damaging to the wheat
(the kingdom). He seemed certain that in a future
age there would be a judgement, but in the present
we must content ourselves with the fact that God's
kingdom is all around, wherever God reigns and
has authority.

This teaching is as old as the hills, but is so
readily forgotten by us, isn't it? We want sim-
pler categories. We find it easier to see a church
service as an expression of God's kingdom and a
game at Shea Stadium as falling outside the kingdom. But let me put it to you this way: surely a
night at the stadium can be an entirely kingdom-
like experience.

I spent a night in the grandstand once waiting
for the rain to stop before the game could begin. I
was cold and I recall the tiered seating smelled of
stale beer and mustard, but I still found something
there to remind me of God's grace. I heard it in the
laughter of the waiting fans. I saw it in the sheets of
rain that sliced across the green baseball diamond
way below us, illuminated by the stadium lighting.
I felt it on my shoulder when my American friend
hugged me and laughingly apologized again for
the frightful weather. "The game should start any
minute now," he giggled, as the thunder crashed
over New York City.

But when you enjoy a perfect day at a baseball game—whether it's a Little League game or the World Series—when it's eighty degrees, cooled by a slight breeze, you can even more easily be filled with a sense of gratitude for God's good creation. Even as the melting ice waters down your Coke and the ketchup on your son's hot dog drips onto your shoes, those with eyes to see can thank God for many mercies.

For a Christian person whose eyes have been opened by faith to God's creative agency—God's kingdom, in this world—such a perfect day would be nothing short of a reminder and an intoxicating experience of God's grace and rule in the lives of the faithful. It occurs to me that this is entirely in keeping with the concerns of the kingdom: peace, love, and hope.

Now let's consider another scenario: going to church. Imagine for a moment that you go to church filled with a sense of bitterness and resentment toward someone who'll be there, maybe even the minister. Consider what it's like to go to church preoccupied with spite because the music is not as you'd have it or the preaching isn't interesting (or biblical or helpful) enough. Reflect on the impact of feeling alienated, rejected, or betrayed by the people who attend the same church service.

The sense of defeat or anxiety or rage can be so debilitating as to freeze you in apathy. Churches can be places where frightened and lazy people remain stuck in their fear and laziness. In other words, an experience many people consign to the realm of the sacred can in fact be operating in such a way as to limit the degree to which God's kingdom is encountered. And alternately, an experience normally thought of as entirely temporal or profane can draw us closer to kingdom realities.

The possibilities are endless. God's grace can be experienced through suffering, heartache, or disappointment as much as through a perfect day at Fenway Park. We seem to be trying so hard to "bring down fire from heaven" in our worship services, while all along God's favor is to be found in sunshine on our faces, the sea lapping at our toes, picking our children up at school, a note from a caring friend.

There's a scene in the Steven Spielberg film, *The Color Purple*, in which a poor illiterate slave girl, played by Whoopi Goldberg, is strolling down a dusty lane with a friend. Beside them runs a knarled post-and-rail fence and, beyond that, a magnificent purple hill. If it was in Australia, you'd swear it was Patterson's Curse, but since it was America, I guess it was lilac or lavender. The purple hill is crowned with a deep blue sky, dotted with clouds at the horizon.

Goldberg's character softly nudges her friend and smiles gently, saying, "See that? That's God making a pass at us." And with that, she said a mouthful! That's God making a pass at us. If only we had the eyes to see the myriad of ways God probably makes a pass at us every day. We sing, "Great is Thy faithfulness, O Lord. Your mercies are new every morning." Every day, God shows us grace and favor, but we're too busy to spot it.

Our prose-flattened Christianity consigns God to various categories and often does the very opposite of what it claims to be doing: it limits God's involvement in this world. But the fact remains that it is not God's involvement that can be limited, but only our awareness of it. When an illiterate and oppressed girl can see it, we're reminded that the poets of this world come in the most surprising forms.

Creation and incarnation

How can we see God making a pass at us? Historically, it has been done in two fundamental ways, both of which I have alluded to already: creation and incarnation. These are the chief ways God has revealed God's nature and therefore the chief themes of God's manifestation in our lives today.

Consider for a moment the following question: when God had finished with the creation of the cosmos out of chaos (whether you're comfortable with time frames of six days or millennia is neither here nor there for this exercise), do you think God had completed his creative agency in this world? Or do you believe that even after the completion of the universe God *continues* with creation?

We often get offended by the old watchmaker analogy for God—that God creates the world like a timepiece, winds it up, and steps back, letting it run its natural course. We're more used to thinking of God as being intrinsically involved in the processes of creation around us. In other words, we prefer to take the view that creation, like a mighty wave, continues to roll throughout history. God continues to create.

Well, if we view this seriously, we'll be ever looking for the ways in which this is demonstrated. God's kingdom is a decidedly creative zone. As I mentioned, it's the place where God—the God of creation—reigns and blesses, and is creating peace, joy, justice, mercy, faith, love. If we're part of this great kingdom, then we are aligned with God's creative processes in the world. We are to be a party to the creation of justice and mercy, for example.

The Apostle John was getting at this, I believe, when he wrote in his epistle, "God is love. Whoever lives in love lives in God, and God in him."[9] Look for the creative agency of love, and there you'll find God. More often than not, such creativity is found in the most surprising places.

There's a riddle in the Talmud that goes like this: If man was meant to live by bread, why didn't God create a bread tree? And the answer is that God prefers us to become partners in creation. Rather than creating a tree that bears loaves of bread, God created the grain of wheat, so that we might plough our field, sow our seeds, water and tend the crop, harvest the grain, grind it, knead it, and bake it until it is bread.

Why doesn't God wave some magic wand and fill the world with love and end strife and hatred and inequity? Because God prefers to dignify us by inviting us to become *partners* in creating love and being part of the extension of God's kingdom.

So rather than simplistically consigning God's kingdom entirely to the category of church, let's be prepared to perceive of the notion that wherever the creative processes of the kingdom are at work, there is every likelihood that God is present. When I sit and watch an episode of *Seinfeld* or *The Simpsons*, I needn't feel guilty that I'm engaging in some profane or irreligious activity if I can see such an activity as being a creative force for godliness in my life. If I can see Jerry and Elaine, George and Kramer as needy, frightened, desperate people whose relationships are veneer-thin, and whose levels of commitment and perceptions of sacrifice and work are distorted and inadequate, has that been a creative process in my life? If, when I observe people whose lives I *don't* wish to emulate, my faith is galvanized and my commitment to follow Jesus is encouraged all the more, could this not be considered creative?

The old fundamentalist "Christ-against-culture" model means I must expend enormous levels of energy avoiding anything that might, to use a much misquoted biblical expression, "cause me to stumble" (Romans 14:21). But there is an alternative model of Christianity that takes seriously the idea of creation and the kingdom and sees the possibilities for God's grace to be realized in all sorts of totally unexpected ways. My faith in God can be fostered when sitting on mountaintops or strolling along beaches. But so can it be when watching Reverend Lovejoy try desperately to advise Lisa Simpson how to deal with her father when he's stealing cable TV.

My students at Morling College comment that a lecture can barely go by without my illustrating a point by reference to a recent movie or television show. One man said to me: "I saw the movie you referred to in class today, but at the time I never saw the religious significance of that particular scene or theme. Now that you mention it, I see how obvious it was, but at the time I missed it. How do you do it? How can you train yourself to see, to use your terms, 'God making a pass at you' in these movies?"

My answer is, "By struggling free from the old prose-flattened formulas that see God at work only in obviously religious ways and by embracing a creation-based approach that looks to God's self-revelation all around us."

Ask yourself: Is this a creative process in my life? Is my faith being encouraged? Am I seeing something more of God's grace toward me? Am I growing more like Jesus? Will this, even though it's painful or unpleasant, contribute to my personal spiritual growth?

Jesus managed to model this for us in ways that still, 2,000 years later, continue to ruffle our feathers. He was regularly pilloried by the religious authorities of his day for seeing the creativity of God's kingdom all around him and embracing it in unexpected ways. Called a drunkard and a glutton, a friend of sinners, by his detractors, Jesus was liberated from the old standard religious categories. For him, God's grace was revealed not only in the sacrificial system of the temple, but in the lilies of the field, in the child on his knee, in the repentant face of a prostitute. Nowhere was this more disturbing than in his first miracle as retold for us by John, which concerns the turning of water into wine at the wedding at Cana.

No amount of fundamentalist tinkering can clean up this story. A Galilean wedding was a fairly rugged affair, and for the guests to have run out of wine meant that they were in every likelihood more than a few sheets to the wind. As much as we might like to perceive of this as a genteel, orderly, dry Baptist wedding reception in a church hall, the chances are it was more like a World Series cookout. Jesus is not only prepared to be part of the event, but he even whips up more grog to lubricate the proceedings!

Just about any New Testament scholar will tell you that Jesus' miracles were in fact used by him to "prove" that the kingdom was at hand. A simple carpenter—as far as everyone was concerned—couldn't rush around claiming to be ushering in God's new kingdom unless he could demonstrate it. The miracles were designed to give people something of a taste of the things to come. Healing people indicated that the kingdom was concerned with human wholeness. Feeding them showed that the kingdom could sustain us in times of hunger or doubt. "Flashy" miracles like walking on water and calming storms demonstrated the awesome power of the Christ. But turning water into wine?

It seems that Jesus was able to demonstrate the power of God's kingdom and at the same time to endorse such creative forces as community spirit, laughter, love, and celebration. The kingdom is ushered in all right, but not at the expense of these things. Today, we might leave the party when it gets out of hand, sit self-righteously in the corner, or never show up in the first place. Jesus attends, enters fully into it, and still brings the creativity of the kingdom to bear on it.

But this isn't to give the impression that Jesus just let life wash over him, attending every party, eating with every sinner, and being entirely undiscerning about his conduct. There were times when he was unprepared to put up with situations that he saw as entirely uncreative.

His cursing of the barren fig tree in Mark 11:12–14 and 20–21 is a case in point. The fig tree's "crime" was that it was not producing fruit—for Jesus a dreadful waste. The analogy is often drawn between the tree and Israel, who was also in a state of barrenness at the time. There seems to be one thing Jesus won't tolerate, and that's a refusal to bear fruit. An unproductive tree, a fruitless nation, a destructive religious system, all incur his wrath.

Another example concerns his actions in driving the moneychangers from the temple in Jerusalem. These were profiteering scoundrels who manipulated the oppressive religious system to their own ends. The Court of the Gentiles was the area in which proselyte Jews—converts to Judaism from other nations—made their offerings to God. The Old Testament regulations commanded that a half-shekel be given by every male worshiper more than twenty years of age. For this charge, foreign monies could not be tendered, since they bore the idolatrous images of foreign kings and/or deities. The worshipers had to exchange their money for acceptable Tyrian coins. Naturally, there was a charge for this service. For a religious system that claimed to proclaim a God to whom all the nations could gather for shelter, this little scam was the height of hypocrisy.

Further, there were livestock, fowl, wine, and salt for sale to any foreign worshipers who had traveled far and were therefore unprepared for the sacrifices. Via the pockets of the traders, a great deal of cash was flowing into the coffers of the chief priests and scribes—the very ones charged with the role of ministering to the faithful and allowing them access to the living God. Jesus' now-famous action of overturning the traders' tables and taking a whip to the sacrilegious merchants reminds us that his kingdom is not only prepared to endorse creative processes in this world, but will rail also against destructive ones.

More wine at a wedding is somehow endorsing a creative process. Violently smashing merchants' stalls is as well, insofar as it is halting a destructive process. Spilled red table wine and shattered trestle tables—God makes a pass at us in the most unexpected ways.

But we need a corrective here, lest we get away from ourselves. This stuff about creative processes can be all very subjective, can't it? I can say that watching *Seinfeld* is a creative action in my life when really I'm just too lazy to even think about an alternative. I guess I could say that watching pornography reminds me of the dreadful temptations of the flesh and confirms my choice not to engage in depraved practices myself. We could justify a lot of tawdry or mundane activity as creative if we put our minds to it. That's why I mentioned earlier that seeing God at work involves *two* basic themes: creation and incarnation.

The incarnation, put simply, is the Christian doctrine of God in human form—the deity of Christ. Christians have believed that Jesus is God presented to us as a human. Jesus is then the image of God and the only example to us of how God would live life if God was one of us.

Often young people are urged to ask "What Would Jesus Do?" whenever confronted by a choice for good or ill. WWJD t-shirts and jewelry can be seen in many youth group gatherings. If God is a creative God and God's kingdom is the place where God's creative processes are unfolding, how can we know what these processes are and in what ways can we get involved as God's partners? Ask, "WWJD?" and then live as Jesus lived.

This, of course, answers the old question about the importance of the Bible. How can I know what Jesus would do if I haven't made him the object of my devotion? I can truly know what God in human form looks like only through a thorough and regular study of the Gospels. In this respect, every Christian ought to be regularly re-evangelized. That is, Christians must immerse themselves in the *evangel*, the gospel, over and over and over.

Just when I think I can justify an action I find delicious but destructive as a creative process in my life, the question "What Would Jesus Do?" should be ringing in my ears. The incarnation, God in human form, provides me with a template for gauging what creation should look like. It's not always simple or clear cut. I cannot in every situation be sure I know what Jesus might do. That's the poetry of this approach. There's no simple solution. Instead, there are danger and excitement and a variety of possibilities.

Coming to Attention

$\mathcal{S}$IMONE WEIL, THE REMARKABLE FRENCH mystic who died in 1943, put it this way: "We participate in the creation of the world, by de-creating ourselves."[1] What did she mean? I think she meant that the more we lose ourselves and become like Christ, the more we engage in the creative processes of the kingdom. This is the power of creation and incarnation put simply by a woman who gave up her life at the age of thirty-five because she had lived as she believed Christ would have had her.

In fact, there's a great lesson to be learned, not just from Weil's words, as dramatic and as poetic as they are, but from her life. Many have considered her insane. And in some ways she may well have been. But it was the insanity shared by Vincent van Gogh and Jesus himself, the insanity of the fool who refuses to be buried by the truckloads of prose this world dishes up. T. S. Eliot proclaimed her a genius of the kind "akin to that of the saints." Others thought her a fool, irresponsible, absurd, a fanatic in search of a mania.

Raised in a wealthy Jewish family in Paris, Simone Weil converted to Christianity and pursued a lifestyle so devoted to Christ that it appeared reckless. Her frail and sickly body could not sustain the regimen of selflessness that she embraced in adulthood. During World War II, she succeeded in getting authorization to go to England and there lived as a pauper rather than enjoy luxuries that her family could afford but which the poor could not. Her identification with the needy and her commitment to the kingdom principles of compassion and justice simply wore her out.

She has become important to me as a symbol of creation and incarnation, and she helped answer for me the difficult question of how to embrace them. When she refused to be baptized and join a Christian church, a Catholic priest asked her how she could pray without a church to teach her or a priest to hear her confession. She responded with her famous equation: "Prayer is simply coming to attention."

A prayerful Christian person is one who has come to attention, who has been prepared to be shaken out of the closet of apathy and laziness, who refuses to drift through life without thought or reflection. A prayerful person has eyes wide open, has spiritual antennae up, and is looking for signals of God's incarnational creativity all around.

One of my favorite movies is the Wayne Wang film *Smoke*, starring Harvey Keitel and William Hurt. The latter plays a famous writer called Paul Benjamin, whose pregnant wife was recently killed when caught in a gun battle in the street. He is still in deep grief and has writer's block to prove it. Keitel's character, Augie Wren, runs the nearby tobacco store that the writer visits regularly for his cigars. One evening as Augie is closing up, Paul arrives rushed and breathless, hoping to catch him before he goes home. He's run out of cigars. As he's paying for the merchandise, Paul notices a camera on the counter and inquires about it. Augie tells him that it's his hobby, taking pictures every day.

"So you're not just a man who pushes coins across a counter," Paul smiles. "That's what people see," Augie replies, "but that's not necessarily what I am." The next thing you know, they're both in Augie's apartment enjoying a smoke and a beer, and the tobacconist is piling a heap of photograph albums on the table for Paul to view. Each photograph is dated with a label stuck underneath it on the page. The dates begin from 1978. Paul flips through several pages and laughs in bewilderment, shaking his head.

"They're all the same!"

"That's right," replies Augie. "More than four thousand pictures of the same place. Corner of Third Street and Seventh Avenue at 8 o'clock in the morning. Four thousand straight days in all kinds of weather. That's why I can never take a vacation. I've got to be in my spot every morning at the same time."

"I've never seen anything like this," Paul says, astonished by the enormity of it.

"It's my project," Augie smiles, taking a drag on his panatela. "What you call my life's work."

"Amazing. I'm not sure I get it, though. What was it that gave you the idea to do this, er, 'project'?" Paul smirks.

"I don't know. It just came to me. It's my corner, after all. I mean it's just one little part of the world, but things take place there, too, just like everywhere else. It's a record of my little spot."

Paul is visibly stunned. "It's kind of overwhelming," he mumbles, as he closes one album and

Augie passes him another, filled with the same pictures of the very same street corner. Paul turns page after page, shaking his head at the strangeness of it all. As each page turns, the writer, scanning each shot quickly, is taken aback by this grand obsession. Speedily, he races through the album, but Augie halts him gently.

"You'll never get it if you don't slow down, my friend."

"Whatta you mean?" Paul asks as he flips another page.

"I mean, you're goin' too fast. You're hardly even lookin' at the pictures."

Paul laughs, "But, they're all the same."

Then Augie, the unlikely sage, offers him a profound piece of wisdom. In effect, like Simone Weil, he reminds Paul of the value of *coming to attention.* "They're all the same, but each one is different from every other one. You've got your bright mornings, your dark mornings. You've got your summer light and your autumn light." As Augie speaks, one photograph after another flashes across the screen. "You've got your weekdays and your weekends. You've got your people in overcoats and galoshes and your people in T-shirts and shorts. Sometimes the same people, sometimes dif-

36

ferent ones. Sometimes the different ones become the same and the same ones disappear. The earth revolves around the sun and every day the light from the sun hits the earth at a different angle."

Paul stops turning pages. He looks at Augie and sucks on his cigar. "Slow down, huh?"

"That's right, workin' man. You know how it is. Tomorrow and tomorrow and tomorrow. Time keeps its pretty pace."

Paul sighs deeply, then takes a breath and looks intently at one of the pictures. Then another and another. Slowly, deeply, with concentration. Every shot has the Brooklyn Cigar Company in the background, but the foregrounds are like an ever-changing parade of cars, trucks, businessmen, children, teenagers, umbrellas, limousines. Then his eye falls on a familiar face. His pregnant wife.

"Jesus. Look! It's Ellen!"

"Yeah, that's right," says Augie leaning across to see her. "She's in quite a few from that year. Must have been on her way to work."

"It's Ellen!" gasps Paul, choking back tears. "Look at her. Look at my sweet darling."

Paul dissolves into tears, his grief flowing like a torrent. He slumps over the albums on the laminex topped table and sobs inconsolably, and Augie drapes his arm around his newfound friend.

The opportunity to share this precious moment together was possible only when Paul slowed down and took a good hard look at something he had dismissed as mundane or uninteresting. This is how it is with many of us. We're too busy avoiding the mundane, interested only in the extraordinary. We have come to believe that the extraordinary is the way in which God chooses to be revealed to us. We desire to see great displays of supernatural power or inexplicable phenomena to remind us that God is awesome and wants to be known by us.

But if prayer really is coming to attention, then the best prayers are those that force our tired, cynical, jaded eyes open to the unlikely and unexpected ways in which God reveals God's being and grace to us. We have consigned God to the dramatic, to the remarkable. We have locked God into the so-called sacred realms of church and healings and miracles and marvels.

And there's no question that throughout history God's self-revelation has been through these means. But it's time for us to learn some poetry and rediscover the possibility that the kingdom is all around us if only we would slow down and take a look. Mahatma Gandhi once said, "There is more to life than increasing its speed"—sounds like Augie Wren when he says, "You'll never get it if you don't slow down, my friend."

Every grain of sand

In the fury of the moment,
I can see the Master's hand;
In every leaf that trembles,
In every grain of sand. (Bob Dylan)[2]

"The fury of the moment"—now that sums up much of life, doesn't it? In the frantic busyness of our daily schedules, do we dare to believe that we can see the Master's hand in every leaf that trembles or every grain of sand? Here lies true wisdom: in the belief that in the mundane and the ordinary, the Master's hand is played for all who would have eyes to see it.

As we saw in the previous chapter, it takes a commitment on our parts to come to attention, to slow down so we can get it. We're not examining enough trembling leaves. We're too busy trampling on the sand without a thought for what (or who) is revealed in each grain's simple beauty. God is operating not just in the religious categories of our lives, but all around us as the kingdom is extended through history. We've let the furies of each moment close our eyes and lift all the poetry out of life.

I think the chief problem is that we've lost our sense of beauty, of perception. We can't see the beauty of connections and the wonder of mystery anymore. One of the primary causes of this modern illness has been our Western cultural predilection for straightforward, clear answers to every problem, every enquiry. We've shut down the capacity for searching and for discovery by providing the answer in clichéd forms.

I think a sense of beauty is essential for belief in God, and the main enemy is cliché, in all its forms. Simple answers and prose-flattened platitudes don't wash in the real world, but the lost talent for perception, for finding beauty, for embracing creation, can change your world.

The first skill we need to learn again is how to go searching for the Master's hand, a truly noble cause that requires courage and hard work. Robert Fulghum's book *All I Really Need to Know I Learned in Kindergarten*, which was a huge seller and clearly resonated with millions around the world, reminded us of some fundamental truths. Speaking of our experiences as small children, he says, "And then remember the Dick-and-Jane books and the first word you learned, the biggest word of all—LOOK."

Why are so many Christians so afraid to look? Maybe because we've consigned God to simplistic categories. We're not expecting God to appear in the so-called nonsacred areas of our lives. We're not looking for the Master's hand in our offices or workbenches, nor at sporting events or in movies. We might attend church with our eyes open (depending, of course, on our particular church), but they're glazed over when we attend work-related meetings or drop off our car at the repair shop.

Sadly, so much of what passes for Christian teaching takes all the *looking* out of the picture. It eliminates searching, closes down our options, answers all our questions, and leaves us needing to know no more (or worse, *wanting* to know no more). Just about any institution these days recognizes that the way to motivate, teach, or mobilize its people is to engage them in an active process of discovery. Just about every institution bar the church, that is. Most educational institutions would be firmly committed to the idea that people are much more likely to incorporate knowledge they have discovered for themselves, than knowledge presented to them by others. Learning is more effective when it's an active process on the part of the learner instead of a passive one.

You might have attended elementary school at a time when teachers made you copy down great swathes of information from the blackboard, assuming that the more data that was transferred into your exercise book the more you were "learning." I can remember spending what seemed like enormous amounts of time committing to memory all the rivers of the Australian eastern seaboard in order from south to north and the towns at their mouths. I think, at a pinch, I still might be able to regurgitate this material. It was assumed that memory, rote learning, and dictation would "expand our minds."

Now, however, while we agree that there are still some things that are simply best learned by rote (times tables and the like), we understand that in the quest to expand anyone's mind we must be prepared to arouse curiosity, to activate a desire to search, to explore, to discover. My children in elementary school are taught through active learning. They are *involved* in a process, not told to sit silently while volumes of information cascade over them.

It has been said that the best thing any teacher can do for the student is to activate a search for knowledge; the rest will follow. To initiate a quest for the truth, to arouse curiosity—this is the primary vocation of any teacher. Sadly, too many of us weren't taught this way. We had answers presented to us before we were ever interested in the questions. A lot of what happens in pulpits and Sunday Schools around this country is really just about taking the search out of learning. We're too used to having the answers packaged up for us. We're never asked to look. Our curiosity is never pricked, our interest never aroused. We sit through sermons in a daze, half-listening, lost in our own thoughts.

When was the last time a sermon, a Bible study, or a Sunday School class got under your skin and activated such an interest that you felt compelled to meditate on the matter, to research or explore an issue, to question others or search for your own views? When sermons end, we close our Bibles. When was the last time you heard a sermon that made you go home and *open* your Bible to discover more?

In his inspirational memoirs, Nobel prize-winning novelist Elie Weisel recalls how, in his first job as a newspaper journalist, the editor taught him to write by saying to him: "If you want to hold the readers' attention, your sentence must be clear enough to be understood and enigmatic enough to pique curiosity. A good piece combines style and substance. It must not say everything—never say everything—while nevertheless suggesting that there is an everything."[3] Great advice.

And along the same lines, film director Stanley Kubrick was quoted in *Time* magazine as saying: "The essence of dramatic form is to let an idea come over people without its being plainly stated. When you say something directly, it is simply not as potent as it is when you allow people to discover it for themselves."[4]

Activating a search

Jesus himself was a remarkably innovative teacher, a man who had the rare ability to arouse curiosity and activate in others a spiritual quest. In fact, the primary tool he employed when speaking to those outside his faith community was the use of the parable. Jesus' parables were metaphors or similes, often extended to a short narrative to reveal and illustrate the kingdom.

Remember that the kingdom is operating all around us, sometimes in the most unexpected places. When Jesus came to reveal those places to us and offer hints at the kingdom's nature, he used these intriguing stories.

The commonly held view among many Christians (I have tested this on many classes and in many seminars) is that Jesus used parables to make the lofty and deep truths of the kingdom clear to simple agrarian folk. Therefore, he used allusions to farming and household chores, as well as to such matters as debt-collecting, rebellious sons, and building, in order to simplify these difficult philosophical/theological notions. In much the same way as preachers today use illustrations in sermons to offer concrete examples of the proposition truths they are exploring, Jesus used parables to get his point across about the kingdom of God. Rather than a long and involved lecture on the idea of God's sovereignty and its evidence throughout the world in the midst of evil and darkness, Jesus simply packaged it all up as a word picture about weeds growing in a wheatfield. So the conventional wisdom goes.

But although there is some truth in this view of Jesus' use of parables, it isn't strictly correct. Obviously, many people saw things in and were inspired by the clever and rich stories Jesus spun, and these stories were repeated and repeated by his followers. But there is plenty of evidence in the Gospels that many, many people heard these parables and were none the wiser to Jesus' meaning— or were not the least bit interested in embracing the truths they contained.

The first three Gospels record an intriguing interchange between Jesus and his disciples. He has just told the story that we now call the Parable of the Sower. It's actually one of his most straightforward parables, concerning the different way that the truths of the kingdom will affect different people: some will show no initial interest; others will be aroused by its message but give up shortly after; others, though interested for a while, will be distracted by other matters; and still others will embrace God's kingdom and grow in faith. Having told the story, Jesus is asked a question—not specifically about its meaning, though he goes on to explain it, but about why he speaks in parables.

Here, Jesus gives a huge clue to the effect he imagines his so-called simple agrarian tales will have on his listeners: "The knowledge of the secrets of the kingdom has been given to you, but not to them." In other words, your eyes have been opened, he tells his disciples. Your curiosity has been provoked and you have dared to look. You have slowed down long enough to come to attention and see the kingdom in action. *But they have not!*

He goes on: "This is why I speak to them in parables: 'Though seeing, they do not see; though hearing, they do not hear or understand.' " In effect, he is saying, "I use parables because they have not yet come to attention. They look like they can see and hear, but they perceive and understand nothing of what I'm talking about." Jesus knew that there is a difference.

There's an old song with a line that goes "Look at these eyes; they never see what matters." This is the condition of Jesus' listeners, and the parables (along with the miracles) were part of the mechanism he used to open their eyes. Jesus then, in explaining his agenda to his disciples, quotes from Isaiah 6:

> You will be ever hearing but never
> understanding;
> you will be ever seeing but never perceiving.
> For this people's heart has become calloused;
> they hardly hear with their ears,
> and they have closed their eyes.
> Otherwise they might see with their eyes,
> hear with their ears,
> understand with their hearts
> and turn, and I would heal them.[5]

It appears that Jesus' use of parables was not necessarily in order to explain things or make difficult concepts clear. It's as if he used them to arouse an interest, to activate a search in the lives of people who were fed up with and turned off to conventional teaching. The parables weren't the end of the search, they were the green light. In fact, they were probably used to sort the sheep out from the goats, as it were.

In keeping with the parable of the sower, Jesus seems to be very aware that many people would hear his stories and be completely oblivious to their meaning. Quite the contrary to making a truth simple and clear, many parables were difficult to understand and appeared to create confusion and uncertainty. Jesus seems content with this response! Those who heard a parable and didn't understand it, wandering off unconcerned about its meaning, were left to do so, like the seed that landed on the path or the stony ground. But those who were intrigued and desired to know more were the ones Jesus seemed most interested in—those who were prepared to get actively involved in the struggle.

He makes this even more clear in Matthew chapter 7: "Ask and it will be given to you; seek and you will find; knock and the door will be opened to you. For everyone who asks receives; he who seeks finds; and to him who knocks, the door will be opened."[6] In fact, it seems clear that the parables are one of the techniques he uses to get people interested in asking, seeking, and knocking.

I've heard it put this way: "Better to have people confused and working toward understanding than for them to think they know it all." Those who think they know it all are like the people prophesied by Isaiah: their eyes are closed and their ears are blocked (Isaiah 6:9–10). The parables are one of Jesus' "sorting-out" mechanisms, a way of finding those who are prepared to open their eyes and start seeking.

We have spent too many Sundays in our churches thinking we know it all. We rarely get provoked into searching. We don't often feel at the end of a sermon or a service that we can have any questions. The culture of many churches is such that "making things clear," explaining away all mystery or doubt or uncertainty, is the order of the day. Church leaders today are so afraid of employing metaphors and similes—mainly, I suppose, because they can be misunderstood by their hearers. A metaphor is open to interpretation. It evokes a response from the listener. There's room to move within a metaphor and, therefore, room to "get it wrong."

So much evangelical ministry leaves no room for maneuvering; it constrains its adherents. In effect, it doesn't trust its listeners to work it out for themselves. But just watch Jesus do the very opposite. When a teacher of the law asks him, "What must I do to be saved?" Jesus responds with, "What do *you* think?" He turns the question back to the questioner, ever inviting an active, involved response. He won't simply provide answers to your questions. He'll take you on the ride of your life.

There's an old tale by an unknown storyteller that goes like this: "A disciple once complained, 'You tell stories, but you never reveal their meaning to us.' The master replied, 'How would you like it if someone offered you fruit and chewed it up for you before giving it to you?' "

I hasten to point out that there are, in fact, times when a straightforward question evokes a straightforward and simple answer from Jesus. The disciples ask him to teach them to pray and he does so. A rich young man asks what he must do to have eternal life, and Jesus tells him to sell his possessions and give to the poor. These are so-called simple answers.

But the prayer he teaches his disciples is only a framework upon which Christians throughout the centuries have built in the most creative ways. The demand that he sell his possessions evokes a response from the young ruler that is not simple or easy. In each case, the listeners are actively drawn into the pronouncement. It isn't prose-flattened platitudes. It is the poetry of *wisdom* that requires a response.

Churches, if they are worthy of such a name, ought to be places where the faithful can workshop on how to see the fingerprints of God in their lives. A church should be a place where searchers, seekers, "askers" can do the hard work of being actively involved in discovering where and how God has been making passes at them. Jesus is not afraid of your questions or your doubts or your searching. He welcomes it and encourages it. I've always found it strange that we refer to "seeker services" as being times when unchurched people can feel welcome to our gatherings. I think *every* gathering of believers is a seeker meeting. We are seeking more of an understanding of the workings of God's kingdom.

Chris Harding, an Australian youthworker, put it this way:

> It's possible to learn to recognize the myriad ways that God touches us outside of that which is openly spiritual and we can share these moments with others. God touches us through painful growth experiences of loss and grief, through moments of creative and athletic excellence, through moments of victory over our problems and through the tenderness of relationships. . . .

> Even the shame, doubt and despair of not being the person you know you could be can be the indication of the Spirit's presence, giving a sensitivity to sin in your life. A moment where you connect with a deep truth through the work of an author or an artist can also be the Spirit's work. A virtuoso performance full of human excellence can leave you feeling you need somewhere to put your wonder and gratitude.[7]

Is he right to say it's possible to learn to recognize these moments? I believe so. Unfortunately, the simplistic formulas we use for determining when God is around and when he's not have sapped our energy. We need to dare to believe it's worth getting involved in the search all over again. Also, please bear in mind that this is no one-sided search.

As Rabbi Abraham Joshua Heschel says, understanding religion requires an understanding of a God in search of humankind. The hints we glean of God's involvement with us are God's way of searching us out. In fact, Simone Weil preferred to think of it not as searching for God, but as *waiting* for God.

To sense God's pleasure

In my previous book, *Longing for Love*,[8] I mention theologian Martin Buber's useful dictum that rather than separating the sacred from the profane, we should see our world as a division between the holy and the not-yet-holy.

Buber believed that many things could be sacred in this world if you realize their potential sacredness. He argued that there should be no denial of the so-called secular needs of human beings in preference for more obviously holy pursuits. The goal of the Judeo-Christian faith should be not to teach people how to escape from this profane, nonreligious world to the cleansing presence of God, but to teach us how to see God already in the world, how to take the ordinary and make it holy by recognizing that it belongs to God.

Eric Liddell, the Olympic runner immortalized in the film *Chariots of Fire* as the athlete who wouldn't run on Sundays, is claimed to have said: "When I run like the wind, I feel God's pleasure." We tend not to think of fast running as a very sacred activity, but Liddell had made it sacred, by sanctifying it for God.

In a previous chapter, I mentioned the provisos of creation and incarnation. We can't rightly feel God's pleasure when engaged in a destructive process or in an activity that Christ himself would not engage in, but within these parameters the world is God's oyster. In *Longing for Love*, I quote the Catholic writer G. K. Chesterton in this regard, and it's worth repeating his personal practice:

> You say grace before meals. All right, but I say grace before the concert and the opera, and grace before the play and the pantomime, and grace before I open a book, and grace before sketching, painting, swimming, fencing, boxing, walking, playing, dancing and grace before I dip the pen in ink.[9]

Perhaps there is the possibility that we might sense God's pleasure as we dance, paint, or write.

We need to come to attention, to slow down and reflect on the ways God has shown us his pleasure, but which we have missed.

There's a saying in the Talmud that goes something like this: "In the world to come, we will be called to give an account for all the good things God put on this earth, but which we failed to enjoy." I do believe we need to learn how to see God at work, but this won't be achieved by formulas or equations. It will take our active involvement.

I also believe it's possible to so obviously consign God to the apparently religious categories that, even though you might be a very pious and devoted religious person, sensing God's pleasure is a remote and unlikely experience. I have met many people like this. A famous example in history would be John Wesley.

A Church of England priest, Wesley took over the leadership of a student group at Oxford University that had been initiated by his brother Charles. The group had the rather sanctimonious nickname, "The Holy Club," and it met under John Wesley's leadership for spiritual improvement, prayer, the study of the Greek Testament, self-examination, and works of charitable relief— all very noble practices. In retrospect, they are now believed to be a group so devoted to righteous living that perhaps inadvertently they gained the impression that these activities of themselves impressed God and contributed to their salvation. The idea of God's pleasure, his sheer grace, was an increasingly distant reality as the group's members became ever more pious or "holy."

Wesley had consigned the religious experience to the conventional categories and had been entirely unaware of the possibility that God's kingdom was all around, that God's grace was freely available to all. In 1735, seven years after his ordination, Wesley was invited to undertake a mission to the Indians and colonists in Georgia, North America.

It was to be a turning point in his life. Wesley, the university lecturer and tutor, the leader of the Holy Club, a man of extraordinary familiarity with the Bible, was to come completely unstuck. First, the project proved to be a fiasco. Wesley goes down in history as one of the world's worst missionaries. But it was his encounter with a group of simple German Christians on the ship to the Americas that really rattled his cage.

No two groups of Christians could be more different or more fully illustrate the gulf that exists between those who sense God's pleasure and those who don't than the Moravian Christians on board the *Simmonds*, bound for Georgia, and the members of the Holy Club of Oxford. As they crossed the Atlantic, the dreadful storms that lashed at the *Simmonds* so frightened John Wesley that he felt sure he was about to die.

The experience was genuinely terrifying for him and resulted in a crisis of faith. If he was so certain of God's mercy toward him, why was he so afraid of death? The terror that overwhelmed him was not only the sheer terror of the storm, but the fear of a man who could not trust God. At one point, he and his English friends from the Holy Club were in worship with the German Christians when a squall hit the ship so suddenly it rocked them violently. The English Christians panicked and screamed as if they were about to die. But the Germans sang on, their simple psalm uninterrupted.

This moment alone was an epiphany for Wesley. He began questioning the Germans. Were they not afraid? No, they replied, God was with them. Such faith Wesley had never before encountered and certainly had never felt within himself. He arrived in Savannah, Georgia, a defeated and deflated man, not fit for evangelical mission. After the debacle in America, he returned to England and was again buffeted by storms, one of which he described as a "hurricane."

All of his despair at his lack of faith on the *Simmonds* came flooding back. He wrote in his journal these now-famous words:

I went to America to convert the Indians, but
O, who shall convert me! . . . I have a fair summer religion. I can talk well, nay, and believe
myself while no danger is near, but let death
look me in the face and my spirit is troubled.[10]

What good is such faith that cannot cope with
difficulty or uncertainty? The Holy Club, though
noble in its intentions, had not equipped him to
have a faith that sensed God's pleasure in all its
fullness.

If Wesley is a hero of the faith—and he most
certainly is that—it's not because of all his study or
good works. It's because he heard the wake-up call
and chose to embark upon a search, a search for
God's pleasure. He was now no longer content
with the simplistic formulas that let him down
aboard the storm-tossed ship. He had begun to
wrestle with God, and thereby he became a model
of true humility and perseverance.

Just as Jesus' injunction to a rich man to sell his
possessions was a confronting and disturbing challenge, so was Wesley's Atlantic experience. Just like
the effect of the parables, their meaning uncertain,
on many of Jesus' listeners, so was the effect of the
hymn singing of the contented German Christians
on Wesley. They activated a search for God!

We shouldn't be afraid to doubt or question.
This was Wesley's strongest and most commendable

trait—the capacity to be genuine, to never be content with falsity or pretense. He wasn't content with simplistic or closed-ended answers. The mystery of the Germans' serenity in the midst of the storm was like poetry to his ears. He returned to London in defeat, but he resolved to meet God. His journal is filled with references to many conversations on the matter, heartfelt prayers, the study of God's word, and the agony of searching.

At this time, a Peter Bohler, without question one of the church's greatest and forgotten saints, came across Wesley's path and counseled him relentlessly to trust in God's great and wonderful grace. Bohler, like Simone Weil, had come to attention to the wonders of God's mercy.

Finally, months after returning home (he should think himself fortunate it was only months—many others have searched for years!), John Wesley encountered the liberating experience of God's pleasure:

> In the evening, I went very unwillingly to a society in Aldersgate Street, where one was reading Luther's preface to the Epistle to the Romans. About a quarter before nine, while he was describing the change which God works in the heart through faith in Christ, *I felt my heart strangely warmed.* I felt I *did* trust in Christ, *Christ alone,* for salvation. And an assurance was given me that he had taken away my

sins, even mine, and saved me from the law of
sin and death.[11]

This entry in his journal is so touchingly un-
derstated, it brings tears to my eyes. After all his
efforts in study and good works, his eyes have been
opened and the agony of his searching is rewarded.
Christ and Christ alone! His grace and mercy
alone! Wesley was tenacious enough to search, to
refuse to give up until he should find God's favor.

The effect this experience had on him would
change the history of the church. Just as the man
who felt God's pleasure could run fast, Wesley
moved quickly, redeeming every fragment of time
(in his words) so that others might see and experience the grace of God.

You see, it's faith that opens our eyes. God's
kingdom is present where God reigns, and those of
us who've devoted ourselves to his service, who've
reached out to him in faith and experienced his
grace, know what it's like to see God's sovereignty
all around us. But it seems we need some help in
rediscovering the myriad ways God reveals grace
to us—through the word, through the realm of nature, through the arts, in relationships, and in who-
knows how many other ways.

LOOK—*if you dare.*

Chapter 3

To Shudder Properly

I CAN RECALL RECENTLY SITTING OUTSIDE MY tent on a bend in the majestic Murrumbidgee River about two kilometers from Darlington Point, New South Wales, on the edge of Australia's outback. Quite a place! It was the end of the summer and the temperature was 113 degrees Fahrenheit. Not a breath of air—no breeze at all. It had been that way constantly for three weeks, and they were telling me there was no end in sight.

The Murrumbidgee was low. At that bend, on its mainly sandy banks, there were a few spots that, having once contained pools separated from the flow, had now dried up and looked like hollows filled with hundreds of gray-black potato chips that crunched underfoot. Even the white sand beach was scorchingly hot, impossible to walk on in bare feet. On each side grand eucalyptus trees lined the banks, their cream and gray trunks leaning gently over the water. As I sat on the west side, their shade provided the only relief from the unabating heat. And yet not a leaf nor a branch moved at all. The stillness was overwhelming.

This was one of the narrowest points of the great river, easy to wade across. The eastern bank was nothing but a sandy wall topped by gum trees, some of which stood so precariously close to the edge, their root balls almost completely exposed, that they looked like they might topple into the water at any time. Another good flood and they'd certainly join the scores of collapsed gums, their submerged branches black and slimy in their sandy bed, the exposed limbs sun-bleached white in the heat.

This is wheat and sheep country—dry, brown, and dusty. By the end of the summer the farmers want rain. Their crops are in and the heat has kept the weeds down in their paddocks, but come fall when they'll bring out their tractors and plow up the land, they'd rather be churning up rich, wet soil than rock-hard concrete. The fields have baked long enough. But there's not a wisp of wind, and no one's seen a cloud in the sky for a month.

I was camped on the Smith's property, Warangesda, a former Church of England Aboriginal mission. The derelict buildings and the ramshackle windmill at the top of the rise above the river are the only reminder of its former use. Today, it's a rice farm.

When the sun goes down, the temperature won't drop until the early hours of the following morning. Swarms of screeching cockatoos sweep down the river gully at sunset. Their squawking can stop a conversation. That evening, at midnight, unable to sleep in the heat, I waded into the river and lay face up looking at the full moon above me. The current wanted to take me away, so I had to anchor my heels in the sand beneath me and balance my weight against the flow. Even then I was slowly dragged, my feet leaving furrows soon filled in with river sand.

This was a moment I won't forget in a while. The yellow light of the moon flooded the river bank, turning everything sepia, like an old fashioned photograph. The water trickling around my ears sounded like incessant baby talk. One old-timer had told me that this heatwave was the worst since 1939. Who can say? It was hot enough and the cool flowing Murrumbidgee, bringing water all the way from the Snowy Mountains, was our only savior.

The river as a metaphor for God's blessing is a common one in the Old Testament. In a land that knew heat and drought about as well as

Darlington Point farmers, the Hebrew people iden-
tified strongly with the restorative *and* the destructive power of water. It is alternatively a symbol in
the Bible of both God's blessing and punishment.
Like the cool refreshing of the Snowy Mountains
waters as they course through western New South
Wales, God's grace is relief and renewal. But as
those precariously stationed ghostly gums of the
steep side of the river bank know, the next flood
will sweep them away with contempt.

Jesus himself used the well-known simile of
God's grace being like a spring of living water,
continuing to refresh and renew us. All through
the Old Testament water was routinely depicted
as symbolizing not only divine blessing, but redemption and cleansing. If we are from seaside
communities that survive by harvesting the oceans
or from farming communities who look constantly
to the gathering clouds, we understand the life-
giving properties of water. But often those of us
who simply open a faucet to get a drink lose that
strong sense of symbolism of water. In our efforts
to see God's pleasure, to experience his grace, and
to open our eyes to look at his kingdom growing
around us, the metaphor of the sea or the river
might have been an obvious one.

Why did I feel so aware of God's grace when I
was lying in that river, when I don't sense it after

turning on the air conditioner in my office? How come we feel so much closer to God on a headland overlooking the ocean than on a suburban street in a major city? The answer is that we know that only God could create so marvelous a thing as the Murrumbidgee River.

Awe and reverence

Since we're opening our eyes and looking at the various ways God's hand is revealed in our world and our lives, we might as well begin at the obvious. God is revealed through the *created order*. To be sure, this is a view that's as old as the hills themselves. But we have worked systematically, it seems, for the last several hundred years to minimize the effect that natural beauty has on us. We have largely lost our capacity for reverence. We rarely have to catch our breath at the sight of something that demands a response of sheer awe.

And yet the need to sense awe and be held by reverence seems to be a fundamental human need. We often search out experiences that take our breath away, bringing us face to face with a reality greater than ourselves. Actually, I think we find deeply disturbing the thought that we humans are the highest form of reality, the highpoint of God's creativity in the universe.

So disturbing is it that we hunger for experiences that remind us we are not the final authority, the ultimate being. I think this is particularly highlighted in the film, *The Terminator*, starring Arnold Schwarzeneggar. In that movie (as in many from the same genre), we see the struggle between the creature—the cyborg played by Arnie—and the creator—humankind. What makes these films so exciting is the idea that it might just be possible for humans to create a robot or another machine that could outdo us, that could defeat us at our own game. Deep down inside, we know that machines are created to do our bidding, to be subservient to us, to serve us. Whenever we imagine that a machine could make us serve it, we become anxious because it reverses the normal order of things.

This is the anxiety that science fiction filmmakers and novelists are playing on. In *The Terminator*, the cyborg just keeps coming back. Every time you think it's been destroyed it resurrects itself from the flames and keeps tracking the humans down. The filmmaker is playing with us: what if a machine—a *creature*—is greater than its creator?

Of course, in every one of these books or films, the humans triumph. The alternative would be unthinkable. We have to remind ourselves through the telling and retelling of these stories that a creature can simply never triumph over its Creator. Likewise with our awareness of the Creator of humankind. We feel drawn to observe sunsets or full moons, to laze by river bends, or to sit on mountaintops because the majesty of the nature reminds us that there must be a force in the universe greater than we.

Elie Weisel tells the story of how the famous conductor Toscanini, on his first tour of the U.S., was taken to a lookout on the edge of the Grand Canyon. As he stood looking into the extraordinary landform created by the Colorado River, he paused in silence for a long time before finally bursting into dramatic applause. So magnificent an example of creation was this that it required the most reverent and yet enthusiastic response Toscanini himself could have imagined: applause.

The Grand Canyon, the Murrumbidgee River, a sunset over the Blue Ridge Mountains, the Amazon River, the Great Barrier Reef—why must we applaud them? Because they tell us we are not the greatest force in the universe. There is something greater, more breathtaking than we: our Creator. John Calvin urges us "not to pass over, with ungrateful unattention or oblivion, those glorious perfections which God manifests in his creatures."

With masterly understatement, he is really telling us to praise God. To do so is to make the most appropriate response we can to encountering the created order.

Some years ago, a couple of southern right whales were spotted off the coast of Sydney. These magnificent creatures are rare in such waters, so there was quite a fuss made of them by those who concern themselves with ocean life. They were made welcome by beach users and so proceeded to loll their way up the coast, calling on just about every Sydney beach on their way.

I was astounded by the response of such a busy, cynical city as Sydney to these animals. Each headland they passed on their slow and casual journey north was crammed with sightseers aiming their cameras and binoculars at the big black objects in the water. It occurred to me that the two weeks we spent watching them, with every evening news broadcast following their every move, was just like a great collective sigh. We needed our breath to be taken away. We needed an awe experience to elevate us from our jaded self-centered belief that we are the masters of the universe.

Those two whales reminded us that there are greater, more awesome realities than our own. You watch, next time you visit your local zoo, which animals are the most popular; without exception they are the great and frightening creatures like the big cats, the elephants and bears, the crocodiles and alligators. This is because we need to observe a creature that reminds us of our inadequacy. It gives us the message that we are not the ultimate power, that there are creatures bigger and stronger than ourselves, creatures we didn't make and who are not subject to our control. Of course, the irony is that they are caged and docile. But our souls are often starved for that sense of awe, that encounter with grandeur that helps us find our real place in the universe.

This reminds me of the song by Australian singer Nicky Chiswell about the "heretical" discovery by Copernicus that the earth in fact revolves around the sun and not vice versa:

> It's like Copernicus,
> At the very moment when it dawned upon his
> mind,
> "we've been wrong—now at last I see it,
> we are not the center of it all."[1]

Well, no, we are not the center of it all, and as much as we might act as though we were, at a deeper psycho-spiritual level, we need to be reminded that we're not.

In days gone by, the church fulfilled this need. When people met for worship in cathedrals with grand high ceilings and breathtaking stained glass windows and wonderful architecture and sculpture, there was a clear signal given to the faithful: God is majestic, huge, and overwhelming; we are small and inconsequential. The cathedral put things in perspective. It reminded us that there are realities greater than we, that God is awesome and worthy of our worship. The presence of gravestones on the church's front lawn reminded the faithful of the transitory nature of life. Worship was an awe experience. It gave us a place to put our reverence for the holy.

In the 1970s and beyond, the church began to change dramatically in this respect. By this stage the post-war generation known as the Baby Boomers started to make their presence felt. As an enormous generation, the Boomers suffered from a sense that they never really mattered as individuals. Their schools were packed, advertisers catered to the great throngs of young people, the word "teenager" was coined as a collective term, young people felt like a number among so many their own age. As a group they had great clout, but they each yearned for individual attention and self-esteem.

Rabbi Harold Kushner, whose own religious community has struggled with the same trends, takes up the story. Speaking to Baby Boomers, he says:

The churches and synagogues recognized . . . your spiritual longing to be told you mattered, that your presence or absence made a difference to somebody, and they shifted their focus from the majesty of God to the sacredness and importance of the individual. Emphasis on person-to-person relationships, on the difference one person can make, became important precisely because it was so rare elsewhere in our society.[2]

So, as a result, the churches lowered their ceilings and threw out their pews. They moved out of the cathedrals and developed the "boutique church," modeled on the seminar meeting room, with plush seating, gray carpets and apricot-colored walls. The lighting was subdued and the coffee was percolating during the short service. The church emphasized "meeting your needs" and began catering to the whims of its adherents. All this might seem reasonable—except that there was a cost to individualizing the worship experience. In the process of celebrating the individual, the majesty of God and the reverence due him somehow got lost.

Recently in Hobart, I dropped into St. David's Anglican Cathedral, one of my favorite church buildings. Though undoubtedly grand and majestic, St. David's is nonetheless small enough to feel strangely intimate. There I heard two angelic

To Shudder Properly

voices pealing through the building, filling the room up to its high ceiling, winding their ways around the sandstone pillars.

It was a midweek afternoon and, as I approached the front of the cathedral, I saw two women standing in the dome of the nave singing an old hymn and harmonizing beautifully. It was breathtaking. Later, I asked them if they worshiped at the cathedral, and they told me they were German tourists and not regular churchgoers. But they had learnt the hymn as children and the acoustics in the church were superb.

> "This is the way churches were meant to be," one of them smiled. "Awesome!" I was inclined to agree.

I am not meaning to suggest we should all build cathedral-style buildings. We can have awe experiences in less than awesome spaces. It's just that too many church services don't inspire reverence or awe. And so we turn elsewhere to encounter something awe-inspiring, something that puts us back into a truer perspective as creatures ourselves. In church we too often feel like the center of the event. Our needs are emphasized, our concerns are addressed, our feelings, moods, worries, and yearnings are the things that drive the agenda.

And we're sick of it! We desire a *worship experience* that takes our breath away, that leads us into

71

the presence of the majestic and awesome God of creation. I think this, in no small measure, accounts for the dramatic growth of the Pentecostal church movement. If for no other reason (though there are other reasons), people are attracted to Pentecostal churches to meet their inner yearning for a transcendent experience that makes them feel small and God seem big.

I agree with American author Garrison Keillor when he says: "If you can't go to church and, for at least a moment, be given transcendence; if you can't go to church and pass briefly from this life to the next; then I can't see why anyone should go. Just a brief moment of transcendence causes you to come out of church a changed person."

Watching whales off the coast, hearing a coyote howl in the middle of the night, encountering the power of an unexpected summer thunderstorm—these experiences remind us of our smallness and of the wonderful largeness of the one who created them. Of course, I don't mean to imply that only the dramatic and spectacular images of God's design should thrill us.

As I write these words, I look outside my office window and see glistening rain drops perched on the leaves of a rose bush. They shine like sequins on a deep, green pillow. A yellow rose bud stands straight to attention, its closed petals dotted with rain drops. Is this God revealing his grace to me? Is God showing me his hand and reminding me of the delicacy of his love and interest? Is God reminding me that no matter how far I might advance as a human being, I can never create anything so sublime or perfect as that rose bud?

In Perth recently, the premier of Western Australia announced that his government would construct an artificial reef just off the coast at Cottesloe Beach, one of the city's most popular summer spots. The purpose of this reef was to approximate the impact that coral reefs have on surfing beaches in south east Asia—in particular, parts of Indonesia. When the swell moves on shore at these beaches, the ocean strikes the coral reefs at certain angles and the waves peel off through deep channels, causing the perfectly formed tubes that surfers love so much.

Cottesloe has no such reef, and the surfing beaches of Perth city are not noted as producing great waves—unless, that is, a fake reef was built underwater at a particular distance from the beach, at a uniform height under the surface and at a specific angle to the shoreline. Then perfect surf would peel off the reef and roll onto the beach, ensuring the maximum surfing conditions for the residents of Perth.

Amazingly, some of the greatest opponents to this proposal come from the surfing community. Surfers are against any such reef being built for a couple of reasons. First, if Cottesloe produced perfect surf every day, the beach would be packed and you wouldn't be able to get on. But second, and more interestingly from my point of view, surfers oppose the idea because they believe it would take all the mystery and the sense of transcendence out of surfing.

Part of the fulfillment that people derive from surfing comes from the search for the perfect wave, not just the riding of it. The uncertainty, the wonder, the yearning—these are important components in the sport. If you knew every single wave was going to roll in perfectly, a lot of the enjoyment would be lost.

We don't want to imitate nature. We don't want to produce rose buds or barrel-shaped waves or any other natural wonder for that matter. Our enjoyment of them comes from our awareness that they put us in our place, a place we know we really belong.

Vincent van Gogh once said in a letter to his brother, "All nature seems to speak. As for me, I cannot understand why everybody does not see it or feel it; nature or God does it for everyone who has eyes and ears and a heart to understand."

Learning to shudder properly

One of my favorite places in the world is the region of eastern North Carolina called the Outer Banks. Here, three sandy barrier islands ring the Albermarle and Pamlico Sounds to create an eerily peaceful body of water protected from the furies of the Atlantic Ocean. That's what they are: barriers.

Almost nothing but sand, the long fingers of land stretch along the coast forming a strange harbor into which the Currituck, the Neuse, the Tar, and the Chowan Rivers flow. Several towns have sprung up on these sandy banks, the best known being Nags Head, Kill Devil Hills, and, most famous of all, Kitty Hawk, where the Wright Brothers first took flight.

Now remember these are sand barriers, formed by a complex of geological processes. Since the sea level is continuing to rise around one foot every one hundred years, this means a retreat of the shoreline of fifty to two hundred feet per century. As the barrier islands are being eaten away by the tide, another effect of the sea's movement occurs. Tidal shifts are moving the sand from one end of the islands to the other. In other words, they are slowly moving south as sand at the north end is gradually swept through the sound and deposited on the south.

Wind is also a factor. The huge sand dune that the Wright Brothers utilized in their experiments with flight is no longer in the position it was when they were tooling around with flying machines. All this is to say that these are very fragile land formations.

The waterway that separates two of the islands is called Oregon Inlet. At this point, the state has built a large arched concrete bridge connecting Bodie and Hatteras Islands. As you drive over it you see huge barges and cranes littering the mouth of the inlet.

"What are they doing there?" I asked my host, and the answer was comical and tragic at the same time. Since the bridge was built, they have discovered the gradual shift in the shoreline is moving the islands south. This means that, if left to their own devices, the islands will eventually drift apart and the bridge will fall into the sea. So they are moving the sand from the southern end of one island and replacing it on the northern end of the other at the same rate that the tide is taking it away. It is costing them millions of dollars every year to nullify the effects of nature.

Watching those barges and cranes and pumps operating furiously to "keep" the islands in place made me laugh out loud. The tide keeps its pace. Time marches on. The shoreline keeps shifting. I often wonder whether letting the bridge tumble into the sea wouldn't form an important monument to the power of God's creation, a testimony to the folly of humankind. Of the seven "wonders" of the ancient world, only one remains. The sea, the desert, time, and tides have taken the others. Who do we think we are?

I watched the sound drain out through Oregon Inlet and combine with the mighty Atlantic Ocean, its dark green swirl hinting at its destination beyond the shore, and thought of Psalm 8: "When I behold the work of your fingers, what is man that you are mindful of him?"[3]

Rudolph Otto, a German theologian, writing earlier this century listed a number of responses normally associated with an awe-encounter with God. They include a sense of majesty, God's unapproachability, a feeling of fascination—including both fear and attraction. He also speaks of a feeling that can never be adequately described, only experienced—the feeling that we are important enough to be invited to encounter the Holy (as he called it), but that in its presence we are overwhelmed and made aware of our smallness. Such experiences of the transcendent are not only frightening; they are strangely comforting. We need them.

Otto, in 1917, claimed that "Modern man cannot even shudder properly." I agree, but we need so desperately to shudder that we seek out such experiences of the "Holy" in films, on roller coasters, at concerts, as well as in encounters with nature. Every concert has to be more breathtaking than the last, every horror film has to be scarier than the last.

If only we knew what it was we are yearning for. We could see that our search is for God's comforting, yet frightening, presence. We desire God to take our breath away, to put us back in our place, to open our eyes and bring us to attention.

The God of glory thunders

> The voice of the LORD is over the waters;
>   The God of glory thunders,
>   The LORD thunders over the mighty waters.
> The voice of the LORD is powerful;
>   The voice of the LORD is majestic.
>
> (Psalm 29:3–4; NIV)

Both the Hebrews and the Christians have been very cautious about ever appearing to worship nature itself. Their concern has been to see, in the created order, the hand of the Creator behind it. Sacralizing nature—seeing creation as divine in and of itself—has been considered a heresy throughout the ages. Worshiping idols, creations themselves, rather than the Creator, is frowned upon in the Bible. In fact, I believe idol worship is ultimately boring. We are simply worshiping our own handiwork. There is no awe, no encounter with the Holy.

Some time back my family and I took a tour of the Sydney Observatory with another family who are neither churchgoers nor particularly interested in Christianity. Our daughters are friends at school. The Observatory is a grand old sandstone building with two domed observation towers, each equipped with telescopes. There you peer through the antique telescope and the computerized one and transcend time and space and lock onto images that are so far away it makes your head spin. You encounter history, beauty, majesty, wonder, stars, planets, solar systems, sandstone, and bronze. Afterwards, we couldn't stop talking about God. He was the most natural topic of conversation. We had become insignificant.

In fact, C. S. Lewis once remarked that this almost comforting awareness of God's awesome might as displayed in creation is a uniquely human experience:

> For the beasts can't appreciate it and the angels are, I suppose, pure intelligences. They understand colors and tastes better than our greatest scientists; but have they retinas or palates? I fancy the "beauties of nature" are a secret God

has shared with us alone. That may be one of the reasons why we were made.[4]

If the raging sea points me to the power and majesty of God, I have come to attention. If the constellation of stars on a clear night draws from my lips the declaration "the God of glory thunders," I have come to attention. But we're too busy these days. We have forgotten how to shudder. Dik Browne's cartoon strip *Hagar the Horrible* once pointed this out to me. One strip shows a character kneeling to pray, saying to God, "It's not easy to believe in you, God. We never see you. How come you never show yourself? How do we know you even exist . . . ?"

At this point a flower springs to life next to him and a volcano erupts in the distance. An eclipse of the sun turns the sky black and a star shoots across the stratosphere. A tidal wave crashes over him, lightning cracks, a bush begins to burn, a stone rolls away from the entrance to a tomb. He pulls himself from the mud, dripping wet, surrounded by darkness, as stars die light years away.

> "Okay, okay . . ." he mumbles. "I give up. Every time I bring up this subject, all we get is interruptions."

Once I was flying over Tanzania in eastern Africa flipping through an in-flight magazine when the captain announced that if we looked out the left side of the plane we could see Mount Kilimanjaro. I have been on planes in Africa and heard this announcement before and have never been able to see the enormous cone-like mountain for all the clouds, or heat-haze on the horizon, so I was a little reticent to follow his advice. But lazily I looked up from the magazine's advertisements for perfumes and luggage and glanced out the small cabin window only to see the extraordinary sight of the volcanic peak just ahead of us.

As we approached the continually snowcapped mountain it became apparent we were going to fly right over it. There is nothing like this scene. Massive Kilimanjaro is covered in pristine white snow while all around it, way below on the African plains, it is green and brown. As we passed over, I looked right into the crater and remembered Hemingway's *The Snows of Kilimanjaro* where a flight over the mountain itself is used as a metaphor for death (and afterlife?). My magazine hit the cabin floor. No advertisement or special offer could tempt me now. God was commanding my attention. It was a sublime interruption.

But perhaps it's the very interruptions that we ought to be looking at. I spoke this way at a meeting once and described how, in Bali at sunset, all the shopkeepers and restaurateurs close their premises and pour down onto Kuta Beach simply to watch the last golden moments of the day before the sun disappears over the sea. A man rang me some days later to say that on his way home through suburban Sydney, west on Windsor Road toward the Blue Mountains, he noticed the deep orange sun setting over the dark gray-blue hills as if for the first time.

"I work in Sydney and drive west toward the mountains every afternoon at that time, and I'd never even looked to see the sunset before," he said. He went on to tell me that he pulled over to watch the sun disappear into the darkness.

Windsor Road is a one-lane highway heading out of Sydney, and everyone knows that in bumper-to-bumper rush hour traffic you *never* pull over and give up your spot in the grinding traffic.

The shopkeepers in Kuta will take the time. But is a sunset worth it? Is the thundering God of glory worth the time? For those who can't shudder anymore, I guess it isn't.

Chapter 4

The Power of Stories

THE STORY GOES THAT WHEN THE CZAR'S forces sought to incorporate the Ukrainian peoples within the Russian empire, the first thing the army did was round up all the storytellers from every village and slaughter them. Such was their belief that, if you can kill a people's stories, you can subjugate them all the more easily.

Hardwired for story

Stories are one of our ways of making sense of this chaotic and haphazard world in which we live. Robert Bly, in his groundbreaking book, *Iron John*, put it this way:

The knowledge of how to build a nest in a bare tree, how to fly to the wintering place, how to perform the mating dance—all this information is stored in the reservoirs of the bird's instinctual brain.

But human beings, sensing how much flexibility they might need in meeting new situations, decided to store this sort of knowledge outside the instinctual system; they stored it in stories. Stories, then—fairy stories, legends, myths, hearth stories—amount to a reservoir where we keep new ways of responding that we can adopt when the conventional and current ways wear out.[1]

If we could steal the stories from the Ukrainian wisemen, we could take away their way of seeing, of making sense of their world. They would become blind and lost and more easily led—so goes the theory. And it's one I'm inclined to believe.

We script our lives by finding and seizing upon stories that fashion sense and order out of what's generally a disorderly existence. From the bedtime stories we heard as children—which told us that evils lurked in the dark places and the good are always redeemed in the end—to the tall tales we hear through books and films and television: these are the building blocks of our worldview. They are the spectacles of life, through which we see our world.

Often unlike propositional statements, the power of the story conveys more than just facts: it connects emotionally; it provides visual images that show the relationship between things and ideas; it motivates and inspires. I've heard it put that somewhere in our neuro-physiology we've been hardwired for story. There's a kind of narrative imperative—we can't be without stories and we find them where we can.

George Miller, Australian filmmaker, said this in a revealing speech at the Sydney Institute:

> All of us carry highly personalized narratives. They make up the mosaic of who we are and what we believe. Most of the time they are implicit or subliminal, because we don't apprehend life by the intellect alone. When there is an interconnected set of stories, we call it a mythology. When it's shared by a group of people, it becomes a culture.[2]

As far as Miller is concerned, stories/mythologies give us context; they connect us as human beings to each other. Another related term is "religion," which comes from the Latin *religio*, meaning "to connect." Our religion is our way of seeing, our way of making sense of things in our world, our way of developing solidarity with our fellow humans.

We use stories to bind together all the various bits of information we receive every day and therefore to bind ourselves to each other. Luci

Tapahonso, a Native North American, says, "To Navajos, a person's worth is determined by the stories she or he knows, because it is by this knowledge that an individual is linked to the history of the entire group."

We tend to say that most people these days are less linear in their thinking. We consider people in the 1990s to be far less deductive and more inductive in their approach to communication and knowledge. In other words, we are more experiential, more story-related. But I wonder whether this is really such a postmodern thing or whether we've always been this way.

Reading Nelson Mandela's autobiography, *Long March to Freedom*, I'm struck by the power his people's stories had to sustain him as a boy and then through his long ordeal of imprisonment. These were stories told to him as a young boy by his elders. From another part of the world, Auschwitz survivor and Nobel Prize winner Elie Weisel describes the way the Hasidic stories of his tradition, told to him as a young boy on the Romanian-Hungarian border, helped him deal with his ordeal at the hands of the Nazis.

Stories form part of the material from which we fashion our worldviews, so they don't just strengthen us in times of trouble; they order our world for us. They teach our eyes how to see things. They help us come to terms with the question: Does the world make sense, or is it all a matter of chance?

The facts won't prove the case either way. It has to come down to the way we choose to see the facts. Is order the rule and chaos the exception, or vice versa? What stories we choose to adopt assist us in the process of working it out. The story of God's revelation through Scripture is the way many Christians choose to see the facts of the human condition and experience. For others, it will be different stories, but stories nonetheless.

These days, self-help gurus prefer to communicate their philosophy on life through narrative rather than propositions. After several books fusing psychology, theology, and traditional values, M. Scott Peck has recently turned to the use of story with his novel, *A Bed by the Window*, and his travelogue, *In Search of Stones*. Deepak Chopra, the internationally renowned teacher of mind-body medicine, recently released a novel, *The Return of Merlin*, into which he had folded his principles of spiritual health.

The Celestine Prophecy by James Redfield and *Sophie's World* by Jostein Gaarder have been phenomenally successful story-based books, designed to teach either spiritual truth (in the former) or philosophical truth (in the latter). At the college where I teach, our philosophy of religion students would much rather read *Sophie's World* than the recommended text by Diogenes.

But my favorite is Julie Capaldo's *Love Takes You Home: A Novel in Thirteen Delicious Meals,* which follows the life of the main character, Grace Sabato, according to her cuisine. Yes, the recipes and menus and eating habits of Grace and those around her offer us, the readers, little bits of useful insight into successful living. It's a kind of gastronomic self-help guide, with advice like "Never drink more wine than you add to the pot', "Pride sinks gnocchi," and "Truth and oil always come to the surface." And it's all told as a single narrative. Very inventive! And as someone who likes a good story as much as a good meal, I was impressed.

But in spite of this new trend toward the narrative as a means of communication, in the Western world we have long since lost the idea of the force of the story to sustain and transform us. As we saw in the first chapter, we in the church have been suspicious of the metaphor, preferring simplistic formulas to the less clear but more realistic imagery of the story. We "concretize" the metaphor (Miller's term), taking all the richness out of it.

A story leaves room to move. Its parameters or possible interpretations are open and therefore it's considered dangerous to those who like certainty or simplicity. True enough, storytelling is a powerful force and should be handled with extreme caution. But it can be used for very great good.

'Tis the supreme of power

We've talked so far about seeing God's grace all around us. In the previous chapter, we noticed how much effort it seems to take to slow down and come to attention to all that creation is revealing to us about God. Likewise, I think we need to do some deliberate examination of what the stories we tell ourselves reveal to us about our longings and even about God.

I realize that every story we tell in our culture won't necessarily have a "God connotation," but I'm concerned lest we disregard too much useful information by not being committed to exegeting the stories around us. I think they might reveal a good deal about God and the kingdom if we had eyes to see.

Please don't misunderstand me; I'm not suggesting that we should indiscriminately swallow every story and every piece of conventional wisdom thrown at us. As I mentioned earlier, we do hold to biblical wisdom and to the revelation of God through the ultimate story (if I may use that term), the gospel of Jesus Christ. But this isn't to say that so-called secular or profane stories can't inspire us to see God's grace and favor.

So a word of caution to begin with. God can reveal himself to us, I believe, through conventional mythologies and popular stories, but we must head down this road carefully and with our Bibles firmly in hand.

Sometimes, when people speak of the power of stories, they are accused of being anti-intellectual. But I don't feel that this need be the case. Our approach to understanding truth must give a place to the concept of mystery—not as an irrational thing alongside the rational, but as a reminder of the non-rational reality of God. There are two sides to every coin. The Apostle Paul studied and reasoned, exploring deeply the idea that God's grace could be available to Gentiles. The Apostle Peter came to this notion through a dream. No experience occurs in a vacuum, and no insight dawns on us without experience to reinforce it.

The idea that God's grace can be revealed through common and popular stories is not a new one. It has long been held that literary creativity can offer a way through the labyrinth of search for faith. Literature can show us the way.

Keats, in *Sleep and Poetry*, said:

A drainless shower
Of light is poesy: 'tis the supreme of power.

Why do we suppose literature cannot shower us with light? Surely, it has the remarkable power of illumination. Novelist Katherine Paterson said, "A great novel is a kind of conversion experience. We come away from it changed."[3]

I'm never persuaded by the opponents of censorship that pornographic literature is not responsible for some of its reader's sexual crimes. If Orwell's *Animal Farm,* Salinger's *Catcher in the Rye,* or Dostoyevsky's *The Brothers Karamazov* can change the world, why do we suppose books have no power to corrupt as much as to inspire? Many great thinkers have believed that literature can be a means of grace as much as a means of perversion.

John W. Montgomery, in his provocative book, *Myth, Allegory and Gospel,* an interpretation of J. R. R. Tolkein, C. S. Lewis, G. K. Chesterton, and Charles Williams, makes a very strong case in this respect:

> The universal and near-universal appeal of great literature to Christian and non-Christian alike holds out the possibility of a more solid subjective bridge by which unbelievers might pass into the kingdom. If faith can be found mirrored in the great literary productions of the time, would this not lead the secular reader to a new appreciation of that faith?[4]

He goes on to explain that the most common way Christian interpreters make sense of secular literature is argument known as *via negativa*, the negative path. Here, an effort is made to show two things through secular classics: first, that the sinful, fallen nature of humanity accords with the biblical view, and second, that "all contemporary secular ways of salvation are deceptive and unable to solve man's dilemma."[5] Can't you think of scores of classics that reinforce such ideals? Montgomery gives a number of examples.

Under the first category, the demonstration of human fallenness, he lists Albert Camus's *The Plague*, which describes the human condition as mortally diseased and no more capable of being cured than the city in the book that's gripped by the plague. George Orwell's *1984* shows the consequences of the human capacity for utter inhumanity to others.

And Franz Kafka's *The Trial* is the account of a man—and, through him, Everyman—who is brought to ultimate judgment, though on no specific charge. Finally, he recognizes that he deserves this and so does humanity generally. It's a testament to the idea of original sin.

Under the second category, the inadequacy of secular ways of salvation, Montgomery recounts William Golding's *The Lord of the Flies*, John Updike's *Rabbit, Run* series and Samuel Beckett's *Waiting for Godot*. In the first example, Golding shatters the dream that education, civilization, and culture can save us. In the second, Updike lets fly at the hollowness of conformity as a form of salvation, and third, Beckett "systematically destroys all the pretences of redemption-by-works in modern life—aestheticism, altruism, intellectualism, achievement—and sees secular existence as a 'blathering in the void.' "[6]

There's more, of course. Literature can not only take the negative path, but be a more positive expression of Christian ideals. It can provide us with "Christ" images—ideal characters who portray a sense or an aspect of Christ's life and teaching.

I'll never forget the impact Jerzy Kosinski's *Being There* had on me when I was searching for Jesus. Chance the gardener is a classic Jesus figure, as is Prince Myshkin in Dostoyevsky's *The Idiot*. Montgomery sees the Christ image in Conrad's *Lord Jim*, Remarque's *All Quiet on the Western Front*, Fitzgerald's *The Great Gatsby*, Steinbeck's *The Grapes of Wrath*, and Hemingway's *The Old Man and the Sea*—among many others. As we've already explored, to "see" in this way requires us to slow down, to come to attention. Jesus and his Father can be seen in popular literature, but we need to look.

Christians throughout the ages have seen literature as a high and noble cause, a legitimate mode of communicating beliefs and ideas. But sadly, in recent times the church has abandoned popular cultural forms. We seem to have given up and backed out, leaving literature to unbelievers to propagate their ideas. We see it often as secular and profane and have therefore refused to engage in its production. We've even created Christian schooling so that our children won't have to be exposed to non-Christian material. And yet couldn't we find Christian ideals espoused in the writings of believers and unbelievers alike? Wouldn't it follow that the stories we tell ourselves reveal something significant about our longings and our views?

In chapter 2, I spoke of the dialectic between creativity and incarnation—on the one hand, God's self-revelation comes about through creative processes, and we need to open our eyes to this, but on the other hand, the incarnation holds us in check. A process is not considered creative if it involves something that we cannot see Jesus engaging in or endorsing. Well, here we go again.

Which stories will reveal to us something of the kingdom? Certainly not those that reveal something contrary to the biblical record.

New covert cathedrals

Literature is one form of storytelling, but a far more popular one these days is film (note that books of Shakespeare's plays now appear with covers depicting stills from the various film versions). I mentioned that we would return to George Miller, who is the producer of *Babe*, *Mad Max*, and *The Witches of Eastwick*. In a recent interview, he dared to suggest that cinemas have become our "new covert cathedrals":

> I believe cinema is now the most powerful secular religion and people gather in cinemas to experience things collectively the way they once did in church. The cinema storytellers have become the new priests. They're doing a lot of the work of our religious institutions, which have so concretized the metaphors in their stories, taken so much of the poetry, mystery and mysticism out of religious belief, that people look for other places to question their spirituality.[7]

You might think Miller is flattering his craft somewhat. I do not; I think he makes an important point. People may not be consciously going off to the movies for a religious/spiritual experience, but deep down inside that's what they desire.

The recent glut of special effects-based spectaculars reminds us that we're looking for a breathtaking experience in the cinema. All the whizz bangery is designed to engage us in an awe-experience. Further, films seem to be more ready to tackle complex relational issues these days. Film is taking on some fundamental human yearnings.

Miller sums up this way: "I don't think we fully understand yet the need of people to gather together to listen to a story and the power of that act." And he's very right on that score. At Berkelouw Bookdealers in Paddington—one of Sydney's premier bookshops—crowds regularly gather for their Master Storytelling evenings. Invited authors and speakers simply tell stories to the audience.

One recent guest, author Bryce Courtenay, said after his performance: "I think they [stories] are essential to the health of a community. Without them, we don't know who we are, we don't know where we're coming from, we don't know where we're going."

Movies have been doing storytelling for years. In the old fundamentalist tradition, the church might have steered away from film as an evil confection, but we have done so to our peril. Now, there are so few Christian filmmakers telling their stories on celluloid that we've almost entirely lost a whole medium to others. Until 1961, both Protestant and Roman Catholic Churches had review boards in Hollywood, providing consultation on the "morality" of American films. In sync with the Hayes Censorship Code, they provided a Christian sensibility to the Hollywood product.

You might argue they were promoting more a prudish middle American sensibility rather than a truly Christian one but, nonetheless, until the early 1960s when they folded, these review boards ensured that Christians were at least part of the process. After 1961 Hollywood was on its own, and without accountability it has produced increasingly violent and sexually explicit material.

My point is not necessarily that we need more censorship—though I believe we need a rational, far-ranging debate on censorship—but I do think that we were mistaken to abandon film as intrinsically un-Christian.

But of course that's not to say that a filmed work of an unbeliever cannot reveal to us something about God's kingdom, in the same way that a novel by Fitzgerald or Hemingway can. As the common person's mythmakers, movie producers can influence values and change views for good or for ill.

This is not to say that "nice" films like *Singin' in the Rain* or *It's a Wonderful Life* promote good values and "bad" pictures like *Reservoir Dogs* don't. There's both good and bad to be found in each. The wheat and the tares in Jesus' parable grow up together, and separating them, according to him, is counterproductive; it is better left to judgment day. There are many films with very little to commend them in the way of revealing anything about God's kingdom; however, there are also films that are useful as vehicles of revelation that are not G-rated family films.

We also need to remember that no one film will say it all. That's a rather naïve hope on our part—that some film will perfectly present the claims of Christ. Even a film like *Pulp Fiction*, which included so much which could offend Christian viewers, ran with an explicit subtext of grace and conversion. It was by no means a major theme, but it was clear.

When Jules and Vincent are fired upon by a drug dealer they have been sent to execute, all six shots miraculously miss them. What follows is a layperson's theological discussion about divine intervention, with Jules believing God got involved with his life, to save him for a higher purpose than gangstering. He deems this experience to be a "moment of clarity" and announces his intention to quit being a hit man.

The debate between Jules and his partner Vincent, who is none too convinced about God's involvement in all this, is interrupted by a robbery at a diner where they've been debating the recent events. Jules, who likes to quote from "Ezekiel" before he executes people, has realized what these words really mean:

> The path of the righteous man is beset on all
> sides by the iniquities of the selfish and the

tyranny of evil men. Blessed is he who, in the name of charity and good will, shepherds the weak through the valley of darkness. For he is truly his brother's keeper and the finder of lost children. (Actually this verse was created by the film's writer and director, Quentin Tarantino.)

Even though he is in a position to kill the robber, Jules leers into his face and announces that "The truth is you're the weak. And I'm the tyranny of evil men. But I'm tryin' real hard to be a shepherd." And with that, he lets him go.

I know it's a pathetic excuse for a religious conversion, but it's the pathos of the event that's so moving. He is "tryin' real hard"—it's a miracle that he's trying at all. This film, so repugnant in so many ways, nonetheless affirms the desperate desire among some (not all, because Vincent is not at all interested in redemption) to find salvation, to hear a higher calling.

The list of films in the 1990s that deal with redemption and grace is interesting: *Black Robe* (1991), *Leap of Faith* (1992), *Priest* (1994), *Dead Man Walking* (1995), *A Pure Formality* (1996), *Trainspotting* (1996), *Breaking the Waves* (1997), and *Sling Blade* (1997) among others. In all of these films a character is seeking redemption, whether it be through conventional (helping others) or unconventional (becoming a prostitute) means. It seems that distinctly religious themes are well and truly on the agenda. In fact, recently a film reviewer in the Melbourne *Age* ran a critique of an Australian film which used the slogan "redemption can't be too far away" under the banner "ENOUGH REDEMPTION ALREADY!"

But don't think that only this kind of film is dealing with religious yearning. We need to bear in mind that God's self-revelation can occur through decidedly nonreligious subject matter. The rage a filmgoer might feel about injustice, deceit, and cruelty after seeing a film like *In the Name of the Father*—about the Guildford Five, a group of innocent Irish youths who, after being unjustly arrested in the seventies for an act of IRA terrorism, were imprisoned for fifteen years simply to appease the English public's need for retribution—can be an entirely kingdom-building sensation. Might this sensation be the hand of God?

When I was a kid, watching television reruns of the great classics like *The African Queen* with Humphrey Bogart and *The Sound of Music*, you might have thought they were doing me no harm. But in each of these films (and in many more) that deal with religious characters, you find the characters being "redeemed" from their religious life and "saved" by secular romantic love.

Katherine Hepburn's missionary is saved from the mission by sea-dog Bogart and married to him in a final act of redemption (the whole film is a redemption narrative in reverse), and Julie Andrews's Maria—lost and hopeless in the convent—finds her true purpose in loving Baron von Trapp and caring for his children.

So many pictures follow this line: *The Nun's Story* and *Witness*, among others. These depict that the religious life is folly and one must be redeemed from it by the highest form of love known to Hollywood: romance. My point is that just because a story includes no bad language, no nudity or sexual references, no violence or blaspheming, it isn't necessarily a "good, wholesome" film.

Story-formed community

So stories provide us with the building blocks with which to fashion a worldview, and they help us to deal with the chaos of an uncertain existence. We need them so much that we find them anywhere we can. But they can do more than enlighten or galvanize us. Story can create community.

The American theologian Stanley Hauerwas, in his book, *A Community of Character*,[8] makes much of the church's need to rediscover itself as a story-formed community. And he makes use of a literary story to reinforce his point—Richard Adams's epic parable about rabbits, *Watership Down*. I'm indebted to an article by Anglican Rector Scott Cowdell for this interpretation. In his piece, "The Postmodern Church,"[9] he unpacks Hauerwas's scholarship to great effect.

Watership Down is the story of a group of rabbits living in warrens on land directly in the path of an oncoming development project. They are soon to be gassed out of their holes and shot before their land is churned up to make way for suburbs. One strange and intuitive rabbit, overcome by an impending sense of dread, convinces a small band of believers to follow him and thereby leads them out of harm's way. And so begins a journey from their warren in search of a "promised land." Along the way, they encounter two other warrens of rabbits allegorically representing, first, the decline of modern liberal society, and second, the oppression of the Marxist state. Neither of these warrens offer them the rabbit-utopia for which they are searching.

Now, this search is no stroll in the park. They are frequently frightened, confused, and uncertain. They are forced to travel for extended periods in the open, making themselves vulnerable to attack by predators. They have to cross rivers and shelter in strange places. And all along their strange leader is no more the wiser about their destination. Nevertheless, other rabbits join them and the band of dreamers swells. Because of the obvious and terrifying danger, and because of their uncertainty about their destination, the traveling rabbits do something intriguing to sustain their courage and their commitment: they tell stories.

It is in the telling of the sacred rabbit stories of El-ahrairah, the mythical prince of rabbits "whose courage, cunning tricks and quick wittedness delivered his warren again and again from its enemies," that the rabbits find strength for the journey. Cowdell concludes:

> The telling of these stories kept the rabbits inventive and protected them from any false sense of security. It also fostered the mutual dependence that is essential for rabbits, so that by journey's end even the most unlikely rabbits have made a crucial contribution to the eventual happy outcome.[10]

In fact, this is precisely the deficiency of the two warrens they encounter on their travels and what marks the travelers' success and the other warrens' failure. The stable warrens have ceased telling stories. In the first case, they are well-fed, sleek, and fat. They no longer exhibit the essential skills of cunning and speed, interdependence and strength. They, despite their healthy appearance, have become entirely unrabbit-like. What we discover later is that a local farmer keeps them well-fed so he can snare one whenever he wants rabbit for dinner. This is their dreadful secret. They prefer comfort under such terrible conditions—the constant threat of death—to discomfort but freedom in the fields.

The second warren, mirroring the Soviet alternative, is militaristic and totalitarian. Rabbits are oppressed, and life is totally regimented in order to derive maximum production. These rabbits are proud that, rather than exercising the cunning of El-ahrairah, they stand and fight it out with the cats and other predators. They have lost their distinctive rabbit-ness just like the other warren, but for obviously different reasons.

Adams's point is that by forgetting a community's peculiar stories that community loses its distinctiveness. This takes us back to the story of the Ukrainians at the beginning of this chapter. They reflect the first warren. Once their stories were lost, the Ukrainians were docile and easily compromised. But Adams indicates that apathy is not the only response. Aggression and regimentation might just as easily follow. It is the telling of the stories that fashions genuinely distinctive community. As Scott Cowdell says, it is "in the telling and retelling (of stories) that a community can be reconstituted in accordance with its foundational vision."[11]

If we go back to movies, we see this kind of cultural transformation through the change in the stories that are told. For example, in the 1950s smoking tobacco was considered entirely normal and socially acceptable. By graduation, kids were up to a pack of unfiltered Camels a day. The culture and its sustaining icons (Clark Gable, for example) loved smoking.

Today, smoking cigarettes is far less reputable, and our current icons (take Tom Cruise) don't indulge. Change the myth and the values follow. So if the gospel story becomes less and less explicit in the Christian community, so its associated values diminish. I believe the church is in danger of losing its foundational vision, its distinctive character, precisely because it is losing its grip on the importance of story.

This isn't to say that we adopt an us-versus-them model for church. That was the danger inherent in the second warren. Rather, we need to be rooted in our distinctly Christian story and allow our community to be formed by it, "while maintaining a healthy respect for the wider reach of God's truth, God's love and God's action outside the Christian story."[12] Amen. God is revealed to us through stories tall and true, but ultimately we are the people of the Christ story and from that we ought never to depart.

This brings us back to the Gospels. I mentioned in chapter 1 the importance of the incarnation as the corrective to our wild imaginations, our laziness, and our fear. We might find God revealed to us in the most depraved and un-Christian kind of ways if entirely left to our own devices. The incarnation—God revealed to us in Christ—holds us in check. It is the ultimate story for us. I never cease to be amazed by how few Christians regularly immerse themselves in the Gospels. I speak frequently and simply tell stories about Jesus to Christian people who tell me they've never heard such things before. Our näiveté is alarming.

Recently, a teenage girl told me she thoroughly enjoyed Baz Luhrman's production of *Romeo & Juliet*. She wept at the end, she said. No one had prepared her. "I didn't know they were going to die!" she gasped. I smirked in a patronizing way. Who could not know that Romeo and Juliet die? It is a Shakespearean *tragedy*, after all! But she didn't, and that's the point.

For me, she parallels so many Christians who don't know the details of Jesus' life and teaching, not because they have failed to understand, but because they never read the Gospels anymore. We think of it as basic, for beginners. We are losing our story and therefore our distinctive Christian community. To retell it would be to rediscover ourselves and therefore to more accurately discern the other stories within our culture that contribute to, or reconfirm, our knowledge of God and God's kingdom.

At a recent study group I heard a man announce that Jesus was a man with a message of grace. No great sermons on judgment from Jesus, he said. Jesus preached grace and forgiveness and love. "Hear, hear," the group said. That's the Jesus we know and love.

> "Well," I said, "I'm certainly very partial to grace. And Jesus *did* usher in a gospel of forgiveness, that's for sure. But what are we to do with all his parables of judgment?"

> "What parables of judgment?" they asked.

I went through several of Jesus' stories where the main character was under some impending judgment and facing condemnation (the Sheep and the Goats; the Shrewd Manager; the Parable of the Talents, etc.) and the group fell silent. They'd forgotten about those stories, they said.

"Forgotten"? Or never heard them in the first place? We must be careful about caricaturing Jesus to suit our current sensibilities. He's far too complex for that, and so is his kingdom. There are stories all around us that direct us to a greater understanding of him, and we must continually immerse ourselves in the ancient stories of the early church and their recollections of Jesus.

Chapter 5

A Religion of Time

I HAVE A FRIEND WHO WAS RECENTLY OVER-
whelmed by a series of dreadful incidents in her
life. Her mother was dying of cancer and her husband had just left her for another woman. She was
battling against the kind of darkness and despair
that naturally accompanies us at such times. She
told me of a strange and inexplicable event that occurred once when she was feeling particularly down.

An angel with grazed knees

She was on her way to buy a newspaper for her
sick mother. Her husband had cut off her phone

and changed the locks in their flat. He was being extremely uncooperative, and my friend was feeling embattled and distraught. Things could barely get much worse.

Since her mother's house was within walking distance, she was on foot and was cutting through a vacant block at the rear of the local shopping center. The area was deserted but for a man standing by himself in the middle of the grassy lot. As she approached him, she noticed that he was rather unusual looking. He was wearing sunglasses and a cap pulled down on his head. He wore a jacket and shorts and his knees were bloody with grazes. In his hand, he held a perfectly formed single pink rose.

As she drew nearer, he stepped toward her and placed his hand on her shoulder and said, "I want you to know, I saw you walk by and I wanted you to have this. Everything is going to be all right." And with that he passed her the single rose and walked away.

That was it! She had never seen him before and she has never seen him since. She said the rose lasted an unusually long time in the vase at her home. And she is convinced he is an angel—an angel with grazed knees!

How are we to make sense of such events? I believe that in our quest to "come to attention" to the ways God is revealing himself to us, we need to take more seriously the possibility that he does so in the most unexpected and unusual ways. We have so far explored what it means to be open to the possibility that the hand of the God of heaven might be shown through nature and novels, through movies and moonlight. I think it's time we rediscovered the spiritual skills required to hear and see God through the coalition of unexpected and surprising events. God's grace toward us can be perceived in happenstance, the unexplained, serendipitous moments.

You see, while these might be considered bizarre or strange occurrences to some, the revelation of the divine through angels—or dreams or miracles for that matter—is a time-honored tradition. Certainly, the writers of the Bible are very comfortable with the Creator being revealed through creation (as we saw in chapter 3) and in the use of stories (chapter 4), but they are profoundly influenced by the God of history, the Creator who is revealed in events in time.

Whether we interpret these events as angelic, or as visions or moments of enlightenment, or as epiphanies, or as times of lucidity, isn't the point. God can be revealed to us in the unexpected alignment of events that cannot simply be explained away. Some have called these "wake-up calls," times when we are snapped back to attention. Others call it *serendipity*.

A religion of time

The Christian faith, like Judaism—which preceded it and from which it emerged—is a religion of time. Or more specifically, a religion of *timeliness*. The Hebrews, as much as they could perceive God in creation, were chiefly a people who could see the divine in history. God was revealed through events in history. Certainly, there are themes in the practice of Judaism that allowed for sacred places, but God could be worshiped whether those places were accessible or not.

This was undoubtedly the legacy of their own history of defeat and exile. They learned that God was not resident in Jerusalem, because he was still with them as prisoners in Babylon. Sure, they revered their temple, but God proved faithful both before it had been built and after it had been destroyed. No, their God was the God of events, of moments in history.

Therefore Jewish theology is constructed out of their history, and the Old Testament is more than a collection of stories. It is the record of God's revelation through one event after another. God is one who redeems this people from the slavery of Egypt. God is revealed in the wilderness and at Mount Sinai. God follows this people into exile.

Those who dare to suggest that the exodus from Egypt never occurred, that it's only a symbol, cut at the very root of Judaism. In the same way, Christians have inherited their love of the God of time. The resurrection of Jesus is more than a philosophical or theological idea. It is a moment in time. The God of history is at it again.

Rabbi Abraham Joshua Heschel makes this particular point about the Jewish belief in the God of time. For him, the phrase "God of Abraham, Isaac, and Jacob" is semantically different from, say, "God of truth, justice, and the American way," because Abraham, Isaac, and Jacob do not represent ideas, principles, or abstract values. They are historical people to whom and through whom God has revealed himself. In that sense, they exist today. The present is not apart from the past. Their God is our God. Abraham endures forever, and Jews consider themselves still to be Abraham today.

The capacity to encounter God in events, through history, is a central Judaistic tenet. Says Heschel: "Unless we learn how to appreciate and distinguish moments in time as we do things of space, unless we become sensitive to the uniqueness of individual events, the meaning of revelation will remain obscure."[1] I believe he is correct.

Our Jewish heritage ensures that just as God has been present in past history, God is revealed in present history. Naturally, the traditional Jewish and Christian view is that God is unchanging, the same yesterday, today, and tomorrow, but no more apparent in history yesterday than today. The capacity to see in events the revelation of God is an important spiritual discipline.

Unfortunately, as Heschel also says (in one of my favorite quotes), "Many things occur between God and man which escape the attention of even those to whom they happen."[2] It's for these happenings, these events, that the faithful should be alert. We can't afford to let the serendipitous coalition of events pass unnoticed. For therein may be the possibility of an encounter with God.

"If not for that day"

This is an important theological point to recognize: if God reveals himself in time and space, we'd better be prepared to see him in the times as well as the spaces. Two objects trapped in space—buildings or paintings, for example—may be the same, if not similar. But two events in time are never the same. Two hours in a person's life or two ages in human history are never the same. What happened once will never happen again. A temple can be rebuilt. A portrait can be repainted. But a single moment cannot be relived. Therefore, as much as our eyes ought to be opened to the things around us that reveal God's grace, so ought they be open to the moments that do so.

My friend who claimed to have met an angel sent by God to deliver a pink rose and a word of encouragement has made the decision to be an interpreter of the times. You see, central to this process is not only the recognition that God is present in events, but also an understanding of the biblical concept of a *chosen time* or a timeliness.

The Talmud, when addressing important historical events, uses the phrase, "If not for that day . . ." It indicates that there are days, moments, times, that are monumentally important in the scheme of things. These are the appointed times, God's special moments. History is not the same because of them.

Some scoff at this idea. Detractors of the Christian faith sneer at the idea that the death of one man on one day on one cross outside Jerusalem could have eternal significance. "It seems absurd," wrote Sir Walter Raleigh, "to subordinate philosophy to certain historical events in Palestine—more and more absurd to me." Why should one hour out of an infinite number of hours be of particular importance in the scheme of things? Because events are the manifestations of divine norms.

Take the following example: If marriage was just an idea, like the process of ever-increasing intimacy and commitment between persons, what need is there for a wedding day? If Christian faith was just the development of a philosophical assertion by an individual of certain doctrines, why undergo baptism? Or ordination? Or graduation? Or any other form of initiation? Because we know within ourselves that some moments in time are manifestations of broader truths.

A friend of mine, a marriage counselor, said to me recently that marriage was just a process. He claimed that too much emphasis was placed on the wedding day itself. His view was that at some stage in the growing intimacy between two people you can rightly say they are married, whether they have a certificate or the church's blessing or not. He also believed that a couple was rightly considered to be divorced even before they separate or go to the Family Court. They were in the process of divorce, so they were really divorced.

Now, as much as I hate to see young couples being stressed-out while planning their wedding day—usually because they're trying to fulfill everyone else's expectations of the day—I had to fundamentally disagree with him. Wedding days are important moments in one's life. They signal beginnings. We can remember them fondly or regret them, but they are timely moments nonetheless.

If it's all just a process, when can we say a couple is perceived to be married if not on their wedding day? When they first slept together? When they first said they loved each other? When they first met? When they were each conceived? When their parents married? When their parents first met? We can just keep going back down the process in reverse.

In the life of a married couple, their journey together is certainly a process that begins when they met, or maybe before, and continues until they divorce or die and maybe beyond, but let's face it, there was a day that signaled they were wed. There was a day when they became parents. There may have been a day when they were unfaithful. Or they separated. They were days that they can look at and say, "If not for that day . . ."

Process and event

This raises the question of the distinction between process and event, which is largely a false distinction. Put simply, a process can be seen as a series of

events, of course. How can we separate these concepts? Biblical language can be helpful here. The
Bible uses two Greek terms to refer to these ideas.

Chronos denotes a measurable time interval,
either long or short. This concept of the endless
ticking of the clock, the ongoing movement of
hours and minutes throughout history, is often
contrasted with the Greek term *kairos*, which usually refers to a fixed time or opportunity. Sometimes it's seen as an appointed time or a timeliness.
But it can also refer to a lengthy period of time, not
just a specific moment, so its meaning overlaps to
some degree with the idea of *chronos*.

We must be careful not to separate them out
from each other too neatly, because these two terms
can serve as synonyms. The Bible recognizes the
complexity of history. It is an endless stream of
hours, weeks, months, years, *but* it is also a collection of timely moments, of special days when particular significance is accrued to certain events, to
particular times. It's in these *kairos* moments that
God's hand, God's particular revelation, is to be
encountered.

I cannot express this more clearly than did
Rabbi Heschel:

> Prophetic inspiration must be understood as
> an event, not as a process. What is the differ-
> ence between process and event? A process

happens regularly, following a relatively permanent pattern; an event is extraordinary, irregular. A process may be continuous, steady, uniform; events happen suddenly, intermittently, occasionally. Processes are typical; events are unique. A process follows a law, events create a precedent.[3]

This, of course, is not to minimize the value of processes. It's not an either/or situation. The hand of God is revealed to us as we search for God. But here's the other side of the same coin: God reveals himself through the events that display God searching for us! Heschel continues:

An event is a happening that cannot be reduced to a part of a process. It is something we can neither predict nor fully explain. To speak of events is to imply that there are happenings in the world that are beyond the reach of our explanations. What the consciousness of events implies, the belief in revelation claims specifically, namely, that a voice of God enters the world which pleads with man to do his will.[4]

There are moments in our lives of special insight, marked by peculiar decision making, elevated by the confluence of events. There are times when we can rightly say "If not for that day . . ." Sometimes, they are days we regret for our lack of wisdom, our foolish choices, our sharp tongue. And there are other days—like the day a stranger in a vacant lot gave a rose—there are other days when events seem to conspire to bring real insight and new awareness. There are events through which God pleads with us to do God's will.

The Christian's attachment to the cross is not the attachment of a believer to the *object* of his or her faith. Although for some Christians the cross might have become an icon, an object trapped in space, the real significance of the cross lies in the event it represents. It is trapped in time, not space.

I am attached to the cross, most definitely. I do not wear one on my person, however. I am attached to the *event*, to the moment when God entered our world and pleaded with me to do his will by dying in my place. For all Christians, there is an inner attachment to sacred events that transcends mere dogma. This attachment to such an event only highlights our awareness of all other events that remind us of the love of God.

Serendipity

Our attachment to events makes us decipherers of history. We see significance in events that others might never have spotted. Our eyes are wide open to events or happenings in which we find agreeable or valuable things not originally sought after. When moments in history conspire to bring about some new awareness, some deeper insight, we're ready.

In nonreligious parlance, this is commonly called serendipity, a term that was first coined (or invented) by Horace Walpole after the Indian fairy tale, *The Three Princes of Serendip.* The Oxford Dictionary defines it as "the ability of making happy and unexpected discoveries by accident."

Serendipity describes an unusual event, contrary to natural order, that reveals the power of God. Serendipity might be quite explicable, it might not involve the suspension of natural law and order, but it is an intriguing, surprising coalition of events that snaps us back to attention, reminding us of power beyond the ordered, rational world we very often solely inhabit.

You know those experiences, when you put your foot on the brake in your car for no apparent reason and then suddenly another car careens out of control in front of you; when something as mundane as a plane flying overhead or a door slamming reminds you of something you must do but had otherwise forgotten; when two people share exactly the same dream; when apparently unrelated happenings strangely affect the course of events elsewhere? This is serendipity.

I must confess that in the writing of this book the amount of serendipity present has been staggering: quotes, ideas, suggestions, conversations all seem to fall into place. You could argue that since I am very emotionally and intellectually involved with this project, I am seeing everything around me through the grid of what will be useful in this book. But this is my third book, and I write an article for one journal or another nearly every week, and never have I experienced such a continual stream of coincidences.

Serendipity is a term more often than not used for experiences that are life-enhancing. So Carl Jung's anecdote regarding the scarab-dream, oft-quoted though it is (by Joseph Campbell and Scott Peck among others), serves our purposes here. Jung was seeing a client so bound up in rationality and logic that she found it hard to loosen up in therapy. We might say she was very uptight and unyielding. Jung couldn't break through, and their sessions were proving fruitless.

Jung himself takes up the story:

> Well, I was sitting opposite her one day, with my back to the window, listening to her flow of rhetoric. She had had an impressive dream the night before, in which someone had given her a golden scarab—a costly piece of jewelry.

> While she was still telling me this dream, I heard something behind me gently tapping at the window. I turned around and saw a fairly

large flying insect that was knocking against the window pane. I opened the window and caught the insect in the air as it flew in. It was a scarabaeid beetle, whose gold-green color most nearly resembles that of a golden scarab.

I handed the beetle to my patient with the words, "Here is the scarab."[5]

The event so overwhelmed the woman that she dissolved into tears. Her lines of defense were finally broken and she was able to proceed with the counseling. This is what Jung called the theory of synchronicity.

Such strange coincidences and events are occurring all the time but, as I've been saying all along, we need to open our eyes to see them. Whether angelic visitations or dreams or serendipitous happenings, it's a matter of paying full and close attention to the events of life, to what is so ever-present that it is usually taken for granted.

If a scarabaeid beetle flew in the window at the very right moment for me, I don't think I'd be quite as casual about it as C. G. Jung managed to be, but maybe I miss out on so much precisely because I don't expect anything.

The gift of interpretation

If we return to my friend with the angel with grazed knees, how might we make sense of such an experience? Maybe he was indeed an angel, as she supposes. He certainly fits the criteria for a guardian spirit (except for the grazed knees, of course); he offered her comfort and encouragement and renewed her faith in the grace of God. It was a truly life-enhancing moment for her.

Maybe he was a regular guy who, after soccer training one afternoon, had bought a rose for a loved one but, upon seeing a downcast young woman in a vacant lot, had a moment of great compassion and decided to give it to her instead. Who knows? Maybe he regularly stands around giving out roses. Maybe he's insane. Perhaps he was a lonely soul who had followed my friend at a distance before giving her the rose. Perhaps, perhaps, perhaps, and maybe. Who can begin to fathom the possibilities?

Enough to say, it's possible that this moment of grace was a remarkable coincidental moment. Truly serendipity. These are moments in time that are manifestations of broader truths. This moment was the manifestation of God's peculiar care for his downcast people.

Some say: "Who needs moments like this? Isn't it enough that God sent his Son to die on the cross for our sins? How much more proof of God's care do we need?" I can speak only for myself. The cross is enough for me, indeed. It is God's ultimate demonstration of grace and favor toward me. However, moments like the one my friend describes are just inklings, small indications of the present reality of that past event at Calvary.

Let's face it, some events in history are long since gone and forgotten. But certain sacred events will never become past. The Christian faith makes the attempt to overcome the dividing line between past and present. It's an attempt to see the past in the present tense. All events that remind us of God's redemptive, costly love remind us of the cross. They therefore help us overcome that dividing line of yesterday and today.

There is a once-and-for-allness about the cross. It is an event the effects of which are timely every hour and every day. The law of Moses as delivered at Mount Sinai has the same quality.

St. Paul, in his Letter to the Romans, demonstrates how the law continues to be timely, as reminder to us of our fallenness, our inability to please God through our actions. Both the law, which informs us of our sin, and the cross, which informs us of forgiveness, are current and timely realities.

The incarnational plunge

I regularly recommend that my students see Wim Wenders' monumental angel film, *Wings of Desire* (remade into the American film *City of Angels*, 1998), and its sequel, *Far Away, So Close*. Dressed in Euro-chic black overcoats, the angels depicted in these films are seen only by children and are invisible to the adults among whom they dwell. They roam Berlin, perched over the city, drawn to winged monuments high above the subways and housing projects. Their purpose is to attend to the embattled and beleaguered urban dwellers of modern-day Germany. They listen to the unspoken yearnings and dreads of humans. They know our inmost thoughts, offering silent touches of hope. But they are powerless to intervene in our anguish.

The films are simply a parade of human yearning—what's been called a discourse of souls. They capture the emptiness of the technological age, the flat, hollow existence of modern urban life. Wenders has attempted to portray the underlying hope within people of the latter part of the twentieth century for holiness, magic, and mystery. His angels are profoundly limited, but they care. The angels (the films center around two in particular), Damiel and Cassiel, also long for otherness—in their case, incarnation. Just as humans might yearn for a more spiritual experience of life, these two wish for a more human experience. They are, in fact, the mirror of humanity, a reverse image.

Each film deals with the "incarnational plunge" made first by Damiel (in *Wings of Desire*) because he desires a sensual experience of life and second by Cassiel (in *Far Away, So Close*) because he is determined to make a difference in the struggle between good and evil.

The films seem to indicate that in the process of eternity (the *chronos* time of forever), there will always be the yearning for a *kairos* moment, an inbreaking of history, a transcendent moment. Though the films are photographed chiefly in black-and-white to depict the limitations of angelic existence, when the angels become human the screen comes to life in technicolor. Only when they are humans can the former angels *act* and experience, rather than just listen and witness.

Hear as Damiel, just prior to crossing over into humanity, tells Cassiel of his longing for life:

> It's great to live only by the Spirit, to testify day by day for eternity only to the spiritual side of people. But sometimes I get fed up with my spiritual existence. Instead of forever hovering above, I'd like to feel there's some weight to me, to end my eternity and bind me to earth. At each step, each gust of wind, I'd like to be able to say, "now and now and now," and no longer say "since always" and "forever."

To sit in the empty seat at the card table and be
greeted if only by a nod . . . Not that I want to
beget a child or plant a tree right away, but it
would be quite something to come home after
a long day like Philip Marlowe and feed the
cat, to have a fever, to have blackened fingers
from newsprint, to be excited not only by the
mind but, at last, by a meal, the curve of a neck,
by an ear. To lie through the teeth, to feel your
skeleton moving as you walk along.

Finally, to suspect instead of forever knowing
all. To be able to say, "Ah" and "Oh" and
"Hey" instead of "Yes" and "Amen."

Damiel is simply expressing a yearning the reverse of that of humans. He longs for otherness as
we all do, but Wenders has cleverly cast his yearning like a photographic negative of ours. It's not as
simple as the grass always being greener on the
other side. It's a vindication for those of us who believe there is another side at all. (The other point to
note is that Damiel seems much more aware of the
wonder of human existence than most humans are.
By being off limits to human experience, he seems
all the more appreciative of it.)

Later in the film Damiel says to Cassiel, "Observing from above is not the same as seeing at eye-
level"—a simple expression of the power of incarnation. But reverse the sentence and you hear your

own heartbeat. Seeing from eye-level is okay, but we desire a vision of life from above.

Wim Wenders' two films tell us more about ourselves than they do about angels, I believe, most particularly about our own need for conversion. Both angels in the films have to take a plunge. They have to fall, to convert. Spirituality without conversion is a hollow form of the sacred. I will deal further with this later, but it should be enough to say now that conversion is costly and sacrificial. To see God's self-revelation all around us is a nice idea, but those of us whose eyes have been opened to this have had to pay with our lives for it to make any sense at all.

The yearning for more than this

If you're wanting reliable information on angels, you might want to read the Bible rather than watch *Wings of Desire*. As I mentioned, that film says more about *our* yearnings than the nature of angels. But it does underscore our awareness that unexplained happenings occur around us all the time. How do we make sense of them?

That wave of comfort that swept over you in the midst of despair. An angel? That horrific car accident from which you emerged unscathed? An angel? The time you rang a friend on a whim and discovered the person needed you right at that moment?

This newfound interest in angels affirms our general hunger for more than we regularly experience in this exhausting and debilitating urban lifestyle. These days it isn't hard to find someone who claims to have been warned by extraterrestrials or strangers not to get on a plane that later crashes.

Bookstores routinely sell books devoted to angelic activity, and Raphael must be furious that the cherubim craze didn't hit a lot earlier. There is now commonly talk about "souls," miracles, serendipity, magic, and the interpretation of dreams. We're no longer convinced that reason is the final arbiter of truth and that the mind offers the only (much less the highest) form of critique on matters of life and faith.

So those of us who are eager to open our eyes to the sacred around us, to see God's kingdom extending beyond the typically standard religious categories, ought to take as seriously the power for illumination of the so-called vagaries of time, as do the New Age thinkers. The Bible is full of stories of God's people receiving insight from God through dreams and angels. It's time for us to come to attention.

Angels may appear more like conquering warriors in the scriptures than like chubby little cherubs firing arrows, but they are no less real because of it. It may well be that we've heard one too many stories about angels helping people find extra money in the glove box that "wasn't there before," but I think we are foolish to dismiss all angel stories out of hand because of it. In the same way, it's foolish to consign every illuminating event to the modernist trash can of "coincidence."

Likewise, with dreams. Sadly, ever since Sigmund Freud's *The Interpretation of Dreams*, which has always received a poor reception with the church and which is today viewed with great skepticism even more widely, we have rejected the possibility of dreams being a reliable or even viable medium for divine revelation. In fact, it probably began with the worldview of Aristotle, but certainly by the time nineteenth-century science held sway the dream was no longer considered as communication with a spiritual world or with the divine. Even though people still found their dreams interesting, the practice of interpretation came to be seen as silly and superstitious.

This is not the perspective offered by biblical writers. The earliest Christians valued dreams as a contact with another realm beyond the material-physical. To eliminate this idea is to strike at a fundamental Christian belief—that there is a non-physical, spiritual world that exists and influences people through intuition, healings, prophetic inspiration, tongues, dreams, and visions.

In the Old Testament there is evident a certain self-consciousness about God speaking through dreams and visions. The people of the Old Testament were open to divine input in this way, but they sought external controls. They were concerned not to be influenced by the diviners, necromancers, and pagan priests of the Near East. So there is much discussion in the Hebrew Bible about the meaning of dreams and visions and their interpretation (see Numbers 12, Job, Jeremiah, Deuteronomy, and Ecclesiastes).

In the New Testament, the new Christian community was apparently far less self-conscious about dreams and visions. For example, Joseph was reassured in a dream to continue with his engagement to the pregnant Mary, and the Apostle Peter finally comprehended the idea of God's grace through a dream just prior to his historic meeting with the Gentile convert, Cornelius.

The New Testament writers assume that these dreams were sent to them by God. They accepted willingly the idea that dreams were simply one of the ways God speaks to his people. Later, the church fathers embraced deliberations about how to interpret dreams in the same way the Hebrews had done. The church fathers acknowledged dreams as a special event; they believed that these moments break into the normal processes of time and are not to be ignored, not to be dismissed too lightly.

Our dreams offer us clues to our deepest yearnings and put us in touch with realities beyond the rational or logical. What happens within our brains while we are sleeping is still a great mystery to us. We are discovering more and more about the workings of the universe and our own bodies, but we still don't really know what occurs in dreaming.

I'm rather comforted by this fact. We do know that normally four or five times every night we dream—anything from a single picture or figure to an elaborate story—and this dream time can be "watched" or predicted by keeping track of the sleeper's brainwaves. We also know that between these dreams the brain goes right on "thinking," even though we're asleep. There's an apparently continuous conceptual activity in the parts of the brain that do not go to sleep. There is another sort of spontaneous image or vision that occurs in the borderland of wakefulness when we're not entirely sure whether we're awake or asleep. And then there's the waking dream, sometimes called fantasy.

Paying close attention to our dreams seems to me to be a distinctly Christian activity. People regularly tell me about their dreams. Perhaps it's because I'm an itinerant speaker and they expect never to see me again.

Never has anyone told me a dream in the hope that I might interpret it. In every case, the dream has been a decisive moment (or collection of moments) when God has revealed something very special or important. People relate dreams to me like badges of honor, so to speak. They feel almost proud that God has chosen to be revealed to them in their sleep, but even more so because they could make sense of the revelation and interpret it in a useful manner.

Their deepest yearnings to know God's will or God's grace or God's voice have been, in part, met in their dreams. It reminds them that there's more to them than their rational capacities, and God is prepared to meet them in those places as well.

Most real living requires risk

In our haste to explain away every serendipitous event and to dismiss every dream, we squeeze the life out of the moment itself, making it sterile and lifeless, like a dissected specimen. Some things can't ever be certainly known, but their effects can be.

My friend felt definitely loved by God, and I believe that's the point. She felt that the experience was a gift from God to sustain her in a dark moment. In fact, despite the trauma she has experienced, this terrible time has been a faith-enriching one for her, and the man in the vacant lot was one of the many ways God has revealed God's love to her and enhanced her vision of God's grace toward her.

I work with people who "divine the times." They regularly say: "Something is going on here. Things are falling into place. We have to go with it." And things do fall into place. When we see all the lemons line up on the slot machine, we know we've hit the jackpot. I think we need to be less dismissive of coincidence, more open to events occurring that elevate the processes of common day living.

As theologian Karl Rahner once said when asked whether he believed in miracles: "I don't believe in miracles; I rely on them to get me through each day."

In our efforts to notice and to decipher serendipity or angelic activity or dreams or visions, I believe we need to employ the same techniques that I have suggested in the interpretation of stories, novels, and films. We need to return to the dialectic between creation and incarnation. Where experiences are life- and faith-enhancing, where they foster awareness and enlightenment, where they have a creative agency in our lives, we might legitimately consider them to be from God, whether in the form of angelic activity, dreams, or miracles—*as long as* they do not contravene biblical imperatives or Christ's example.

For example, I don't believe an angel can convince us that drunkenness or debauchery are acceptable life choices for a Christian. I don't think any dream that encourages selfishness or avarice can be "from God."

And here lies an interesting dilemma for those of us committed to engaging in the dialectic between creation and incarnation. There are voices calling us to remain lazy or fearful, lustful or violent. We do dream such things. We are tempted by serendipitous moments to choose evil rather than good. Sometimes, events constrain to make it easy for us to steal and not be caught, to lie and never be found out. Can these moments be God's doing? Hardly.

In other words, it is a daily, lifelong struggle to engage in the dialectic. To be forever interpreting events, moments, and experiences is a decidedly Christian process. I believe this is, in part, what

Christ had in mind when he called us to take up the cross or put our hand to the plow. It includes the daily, hourly debate about what is both creative and incarnational.

Sure, it's dangerous and murky. The answers aren't always simple and clear. If you want simplistic formulas, try another religion. Most real living requires risks. Without risk, our lives peter out in dead-end streets. The way of Christ involves the risky, frightening but exciting challenge to live fully and truly, without shirking a fight or avoiding a sacrificial choice.

But as much as it requires commitment, hard work and sacrifice, being a Christian includes the potential for rhythm. Such a constant debate can become part of the natural rhythm of the Christian lifestyle. In the same way that, after years of practicing scales and attending piano lessons, a musician can one day play a symphony with an orchestra, I think those of us committed to seeing what is biblically creative and teasing it out for all it's worth can develop greater mastery and freedom over evil and the voices that call us to abandon Christ's example.

Author and lecturer David Tacey of La Trobe University poses an important problem in our society:

> Religion is founded on a deep and abiding awareness of human evil. I never understood

this as a child, but as we grow up we are exposed to the fact of human darkness and realize that society has to protect itself from evil. But in our world the idea of evil is hugely unpopular; when poets and priests talk about it, they are dismissed as mediaeval or out of touch. Haven't they heard that no one believes in sin any more, that we are all fundamentally "good"?

The problem is: in a world where everything is deemed "good," where the criminal is protected by the law, where [soccer] is religion, sex is wholesome and money is sacred, where does evil go?[6]

Where does evil go? How can it be contained? Our commitment as Christians to embrace the creative forces in the world and to do so with a distinctly incarnational model involves us in standing against evil and resisting those forces that are destructive by their very nature. This is the incarnation.

Christ's death and resurrection is then the model. We resist any dream that calls us to abandon sacrifice. We ignore any "angel" who encourages faithlessness. We refuse to be drawn into any serendipitous moment that prompts laziness or selfishness. And we spend every waking moment looking for signals and interpreting them responsibly and biblically.

To do so, I believe, takes the concerted cooperative effort of whole communities of Christians. No individual ought to be charged with such responsibility alone.

Chapter 6

Seeing Christ in Others

SOME YEARS AGO, WHEN I WAS WORKING AS A pastor with a local church in Sydney, I was involved in a regular weekly high school Scripture program at our local high school. We regularly invited guests to come along and present seminars to the students. These consisted of a variety of subjects, some of which interested the students and others which definitely did not. Allow me to give you an example of the latter.

Being Christ

We invited a former missionary to Jordan to come and share about his experiences in the Middle

East. You might be thinking already that this had disaster written all over it, but for about half the session the speaker kept the group of around two hundred kids enthralled. He spoke of his days as a privileged public school boy from London and how he gave up a promising career in law to travel to Jordan to tell others about Jesus. His wife was with him in the class and they dressed a couple of junior students up in traditional dress, explaining the cultural differences between Britain and the Middle East.

It was quite interesting for a while. But around halfway through the meeting, he began preaching at the students and they became increasingly agitated. They were not *really* badly behaved (believe me, I've seen really badly behaved groups in my time!), just a bit restless and uninterested. It was then that he made his first bad move. Leaving off from his presentation, he berated the kids for not listening attentively enough and told them to settle down. It was all downhill from there.

The students did not appreciate him suddenly sounding like a cranky teacher, and a few of them whistled and jeered softly under their breath. At this, he raised his voice and told them to be quiet because he was a guest in the school and shouldn't be treated this way. They continued their efforts. He bellowed at them that he would not put up with such insolent behavior. He had driven a long way, he claimed, and he shouldn't be subjected to such rudeness. All this only intensified their jeering.

He then told them that the Bible claims that "a fool says in his heart, there is no God." "If you don't believe, you are all fools," he burst forth loudly, and before long pandemonium was ruling supreme. In other words, all hell had broken loose.

A youth worker and I were standing at the back of the hall watching this visitor going hell-bent-for-leather in a yelling match with a couple of hundred teenagers. It was dreadful. We resolved that there was nothing much we could do. After all, as the youth worker said, he had got himself into this mess and he could get himself out. But we couldn't allow it to go on forever.

Finally, I walked to the front of the hall and settled the group down (no mean feat) and asked the missionary speaker to move away from the microphone. I then announced to the students that, while their behavior was out of line, I did not endorse the abuse that the speaker had hurled at them. "I do not think you're fools," I said. "You're pretty decent teenagers who are capable of thinking through the important issues of faith and religion."

I then told them they could leave the class early and dismissed the group. At this, the missionary speaker was livid. He now directed the anger that he had been venting on the kids toward me. "How dare you humiliate me like that!" he screamed. "I am a guest in this school. I shouldn't be treated this way by those children!"

At that, I turned to him and said sternly, "Right now, you're not a guest in this school. You're not a missionary from Jordan. You're not even a former lawyer. Right now in this setting, before these students, you are Christ. You are the closest thing these kids will ever get to seeing what Jesus looks like. They don't go to church or attend Sunday Schools. The only chance they ever get to see what Christ is like is when we walk in here to take these religious education sessions."

At this point, I was warming to my subject and so I continued a little more stridently, "So when you call them fools and berate them for their lack of faith, you show them that that's how Jesus sees them. And as far as I can tell, in the Gospels, the only time Jesus ever abuses people for their lack of piety, he's speaking to the religious leaders!"

Here's the rub. Those of us who follow Christ *are* Christ to those outside the church. There are no two ways about it. We are to be ever vigilant about this. I don't think it means we have to be gentle, meek and mild, totally equanimous, unruffled, serene, and peaceful. Precisely because I don't see Jesus this way.

Reread the Gospels and you'll discover a complex, strange, but wonderful man, capable of sadness, loneliness, anger, disappointment, frustration, and annoyance; but also a man able to express such emotions in godly and righteous ways. The key is for us to *immerse* ourselves in the Gospel records of the incarnation.

The missionary was too concerned with presenting Christ rather than *being* Christ. And there's a difference. By contrast, a few years ago, I heard an associate of Australian evangelist John Smith tell a story about the day Smithy was presenting a religious education seminar in a high school in Melbourne. After the formal input, the students were invited to put any questions they might have about religion or Jesus or Christianity on cards to be read out on the platform and answered by John. Most of them were serious questions about the sensibility of the Christian faith. But one of the questions read, "Where was God when I was raped?"

It is a theological question. But it was also a cry from the heart. After it was read and before John Smith could answer, he began to weep. His friend who told me the story said big salty tears rolled down Smithy's cheeks into his moustache and for several seconds he couldn't speak. The whole group of students fell deathly silent as the evangelist cried on the platform for the pain expressed in the desperate question on that card.

There was no need for any theological answer after that. Where was God when I was raped? The answer was expressed in those big, salty tears. Smith was *being* Christ, not defending him. In our attempts to see the kingdom of God around us and to come to attention to God's small mercies and great graces, we need to be looking to find Christ in others. It begins by being committed to become more like Christ ourselves.

Seeing Christ in others is an interesting business. Sometimes, he's to be found in the most unlikely places. Other times, in the most expected. When the archbishop looks like Jesus, we might not be surprised. But when the illiterate or the disabled reflect Christ, we are often taken aback. That's if we are looking for him in them at all.

All too often, Jesus is presented to us in the form of white, middle-class, college-educated males. We are used to seeing him represented by articulate, handsome men, who are outspoken, goal-oriented, and effective. Sure, they are often compassionate, caring men with a heart for others and a commitment to integrity and honesty, fidelity and hard work. But by being so seduced by these men as the *only* way Christ is seen in human form these days, we miss out on too much.

Some years ago, I was preaching in a suburban church in Sydney. The worship leader had planned an open prayer time in the service, during which any member of the congregation could lead the others in prayer. Several people stood up and prayed out aloud, their prayers being met with re-sounding amens and *mm-mms* (deep evangelical grunts).

The last member of the congregation to pray was a cerebral palsied man named Paul. He was so physically disabled that his twisted, contorted mouth could not form words. He communicated with others by manipulating his quaking hand to point slowly to letters on a board attached to his wheelchair. Saliva ran fluently from the corner of his lips.

His prayer was one of the most moving I have heard. It began like this, "Uuuurgh, mmmh, aaaaarh, uuuuurgh, uuuuurgh." This bizarre groaning rolled on for several minutes. His deep inner thoughts were vented in that church for all to hear. No longer constrained by his twisted hand or his letter board, he gave voice to his full-throated prayer.

To the untrained ear it might have sounded ugly. Some might have been uncomfortable at this long, guttural moaning. But to the One to whom it was directed, it was music to the ears. I felt privileged to be an eavesdropper, to listen in on this magnificent prayer of faith. My love for Jesus was intensified as I heard the heartfelt yearnings of this contorted and disabled man. I didn't really need to deliver a sermon that day.

I guess moments like that one are obvious ways our faith is stirred by others. But I want to encourage you to look a little harder around you for the ways God's love is shining through even the most unlikely characters. I'm sure you have a minister or elder, a preacher or church leader you respect, who models Christlikeness to you—but maybe the woman who runs the corner store or the man who pumps your gas has something to show you, too. To see another as if he or she were Christ can do wonders for our faith.

"Jesus comes through irregular channels"

I've come to deeply respect the great Methodist missionary to India, E. Stanley Jones. His book *The Christ of the Indian Road* is a classic reminder of taking the gospel to others, while seeing him at work in their lives already (my precious copy is a 1926 edition). In it, he speaks of how Jesus has been presented to the Indian people through both "regular channels" and "irregular channels." By regular channels he means the missionaries and evangelists, the preachers and teachers who have affected the people of India with the gospel. For the irregular channel, he cites a surprising image of Jesus: Mahatma Gandhi.

Gandhi most certainly was not a Christian and did not identify himself as such. He called himself a Hindu. So for a man like E. Stanley Jones to say that Jesus had come to India through Mahatma Gandhi was (and still is) a provocative statement for many people. Yet he relates the story of hearing an evangelical preacher speak of the great advance the gospel was making in India in the 1920s.

After the presentation, Jones was speaking to a Hindu who had heard the lecture and agreed that Christianity was taking root in India and who said, "But the speaker failed to say that Mahatma Gandhi was responsible for a great deal of this new interest in Jesus."

Jones goes on to say that, in India, the idea of suffering was inextricably linked to *karma*, to the concept of rewards and punishment. If one was suffering, it was due to circumstances or choices made by him or others for which he was being punished. In other words, all suffering is punitive and the result of previous sin. To preach the cross of Christ and to commend the idea of redemptive suffering was like bashing your head against a brick wall. Jesus must have been a very wicked man, according to the idea of *karma,* to have suffered so terribly.

That was until Gandhi. Almost singlehandedly, he planted the idea in the hearts of Indians of suffering for others as a choice of supreme, noble, self-sacrifice. Jones quotes a brilliant Hindu thinker as saying, "What the missionaries have not been able to do in fifty years Gandhi by his life and trial and incarceration has done—namely, he has turned the eyes of India toward the cross."

Jesus comes through irregular channels, said Jones. Though a missionary of considerable zeal, he couldn't care less whether Gandhi or the Western preachers got the credit. He knew in 1926 that it was possible to talk to the average Indian about nationalism and freedom and for this to form a natural conduit into discussing the program of the Mahatma. From there, he could to turn the discussion toward the cross and the sacrifice of Christ. A door had opened. Jesus had revealed himself in the form of a Hindu holy man.

Jones retells the story of C. F. Andrews' encounter with Gandhi during his famous protest fast:

> On the eighteenth day of the fast, Mr C. F. Andrews, who was editing Gandhi's paper, *Young India,* while he was fasting, wrote an editorial

in which he described Gandhi lying upon his
couch on the upper veranda in Delhi, weak and
emaciated. He pictured the fort which could
be seen in the distance, reminding them of the
struggle for the possession of the kingdom;
below the fort, Englishmen could be seen going
out to their golf; nearer at hand, the crowds of
his own people surged through the bazaar intent on buying and selling.

While Andrews watched him there, that verse
of Scripture rushed to his mind: "Is it nothing
to you, ye that pass by? Is there any sorrow
like unto my sorrow?"

He ended it with this sentence: "As I looked
upon him there and caught the meaning of it
all, I felt as never before in my own experience
the meaning of the cross."[1]

Even the most fiery opponents of Christianity
were swayed by the power of the idea of redemptive suffering. The cross could at last make sense to
them. Some missionaries might have been miffed
that it wasn't their great preaching or pastoral
hearts that convinced Indians, but beggars can't be
choosers. God moves in mysterious ways!

Objectifying others

One of the key reasons we find it difficult to see
Christ in others is that there are powerful social

forces at work limiting our capacity to do so. Chiefly, I am referring to our culture's emphasis on objectifying people.

The great Jewish theologian Martin Buber spoke of the distinction in our minds between treating people as *subjects* and *objects*. By objects, he meant that propensity in our world for people to see others for what use they might have for them. As we increasingly deal with inanimate objects that fulfill certain functions for us, we become ever more likely to treat people the same way. To see others as subjects is to encounter them in a way that acknowledges that they are beings at least as complex as we ourselves are.

Whenever we write someone off as "just an old coot" or "a dumb blonde," we are objectifying the person. Whenever we dismiss all young people as lazy or all non-Christians as godless, depraved pagans, we've fallen for it. When we dismiss the disabled or the foreigner, we rule out the possibility for Christ to be revealed through a spastic or a Hindu.

There is the story of the Hindu man who worked as a cleaner in a grand home owned by a British colonel in India during the Raj. The colonel's wife was having society women over for cucumber sandwiches and gin and tonics one day, and her cleaner had not arrived for work. The circular gravel driveway at the front of the house was littered with leaves, and the front steps were filthy. Moments before the guests arrived, when the mistress was frantic, the cleaner raced up the driveway, his rattan brush in his hand. The mistress orders him to complete the job in double-quick time and then tells him never to come back. He has been sacked.

The Hindu man bent low to the earth and apologized for his lateness. It was just that his son had died the previous night and he had to make the appropriate arrangements that morning as Hindu custom prescribed. For the first time in her life, the colonel's wife considered the possibility that this man had a family and felt pain and joy, triumph and tragedy, as she did. Until then, he was just the man who swept the driveway. He was just a useful object.

If we disregard the people with Down's Syndrome because they have no utility for us, we limit the degree to which God can reveal grace to us through them. If I ignore the newcomer to my land because I can't understand his language and I have no need to relate to him, likewise I limit God's revelation to me. The more I open myself to others as *subjects*, the more I open myself to God. If I base relationships on my needs and do not look on others as subjects, acknowledging *their* uniqueness, then I am using them—to meet my need for love, affirmation, or material wealth.

No one wants to think of him or herself as someone who uses other people, but in a sense, as Buber points out, we're all users if we're honest with ourselves. We have all the time in the world for those we need and rarely any time for those who have nothing we want.

We're so accustomed to utilizing automatic teller machines and drive-thru windows, and we have been lulled into treating people in the same manner. In 1990, *USA Today* ran an advertisement by the financial analysis firm Dun & Bradstreet, in which a full page contained only four brief sentences in bold type:

> I'M 30,000 FEET OVER NEBRASKA AND THE GUY NEXT TO ME SOUNDS LIKE A PROSPECT. I FIGURE I'LL BUY HIM A DRINK, BUT FIRST I EXCUSE MYSELF AND GO TO THE PHONE. I CALL D&B FOR HIS COMPANY'S CREDIT RATING. THREE MINUTES LATER I'M BACK IN MY SEAT BUYING A BEER FOR MY NEW BEST FRIEND.[2]

God help us if our "new best friends" are made based on their company's credit ratings. Our society is in terrible shape when we have so objectified and reduced human beings down to what they can offer us. How can we possibly see Christ revealing himself to us through others unless we can dignify others as if they were Christ?

I heard it put this way: "You love God as much, and no more, than the person you love the least." The more we dismiss another as an object, the less we are open to God's grace. The church can be all too guilty of caricaturing others as "raving Pentecostals" or "uptight Calvinists" without any concern to interact with others as *subjects.*

The way out

Is there any way out of this mess? How can we be freed from our regular temptation to objectify others and thereby limit our openness to God? Well, the question could be expanded to include how we can be more open to seeing God in the natural order, or through stories, films, books, and so on. How can I open my eyes and come to attention to God's kingdom unfolding in my life through dreams and angels, miracles and happenstance?

My answer is found at the root of the idea of conversion. We need to be soundly *converted* in order to be able to get it. By converted I mean thoroughly shaken out of our complacency and our old fashioned formulas. We need a renewed, rebirthed perspective. No longer will the same old slogans and simplistic answers do the trick. This takes us back to where we began—yearning for a poetic faith in a prose-flattened world.

In 1901, William James wrote his classic treatment on this subject, called *The Varieties of Religious Experience.* In it, he spoke of the difference between once-born and twice-born souls. Once-born souls are those people who grow up in Western culture imbibing all the standard "Christian" statements about life. Their worldview is simple and clear. God is in heaven. The good and faithful ones are rewarded. The evil are punished. The world is an ordered, straightforward place. It is blessed by God with natural and logical consequence. When we choose to do wrong, we will suffer. When we decide to do right, we are blessed. Liars will come unstuck. Deceit will always be found out. Dishonesty and depravity will lead to unhappiness for their perpetrators. It's *that* simple.

Every time your parents told you that if you eat your veggies, you will grow up healthy and strong, they were propagating this worldview. When we heard them quote, "Be sure your sins will find you out," we got this model reinforced. Go to bed early and you'll wake up healthy, wealthy, and wise, they said. Children's stories confirmed it. Don't go to the woods or the wolf will get you. Choose correctly and your life will work out. Every episode of sitcoms like *The Brady Bunch* demonstrated to us that when the kids contravened the rules, they ended up in trouble. William James called this simplicity symptomatic of a once-born faith. It might be fine for little children, but it's never enough for clear-thinking adults.

What James forecast was that as we develop through adolescence into adulthood, something terrible happens: we begin to see instances where the dishonest prosper or where the faithful suffer. It doesn't take much insight into the chaotic and haphazard world in which we live to see that the simple formulas we were given as children don't always hold firm. We can say our prayers, attend our churches, stay committed to honesty, integrity, and fidelity—and still suffer all kinds of ills.

The faithful still get sick. Their businesses don't always prosper because they are honest. The faithful still see their marriages fail or their children die. We begin to ask ourselves the dramatic existential question: "Is the world really a safe, orderly, sensible place?" At this point, said James, we enter into a period of *lostness*.

To be lost is to go through the painful and debilitating process of questioning the old once-born kind of worldview. James considered this to be a process that typically accompanied adolescence (he is credited as one of the seminal thinkers on this stage of life), but we can probably all think of people who have led such sheltered lives they didn't come to ask such questions until well into adulthood. I know some who, because they have led such difficult lives, asked this questions before they hit their teens. As traumatic as this questioning might be, James claimed that such "lostness" was essential to embracing what he called twice-born faith.

Many give up on any sense of religious faith and remain in their lostness, uncertain and without real integrity. But others, the brave ones, manage to hang onto faith, even in the midst of pain and suffering. They come through the period of doubt with a very different faith from the one with which they began. Instead of seeing a world flooded with sunshine for the faithful, they see a world where the sun struggles to come out after the storm but always manages to reappear.

Theirs is a much less cheerful, less confident, but more realistic outlook. God is no longer the parent who keeps us safe and dry; God is the power who enables us to keep going in a stormy and dangerous world.

Twice-born faith

Another thinker who has some useful things to say in this respect is the Swiss educational psychologist, Jean Piaget. He had a deceptively simple way of gathering data on his research into cognitive development.

Piaget would go out into the streets of Geneva and ask children of varying ages to explain to him the rules of how they played marbles. Once they'd explained the rules, he would ask them *how* they knew these were the rules. Very young children had no idea how they knew these were the rules. They just *were!* No one had taught them to play. They just knew these rules because everyone else played by them. In other words, the rules had been learned by social osmosis. They just picked them up from older kids.

Children a little older were quite affronted by the question. When asked, "*How* do you know these are the rules?" they became agitated. They had never questioned the rules before and to be asked for the reasoning behind the rules was upsetting. Piaget found that this often activated a rebellion among the children. They would ask themselves: Why should we play by these rules anyway? Often this meant that they would throw the rules out and this resulted in chaotic games, where only the biggest or the loudest won (or the one with the most marbles).

Piaget then asked children a little older again about how they played marbles and how they knew these were the rules. He found in this, the oldest group, there was a keen sense of *why* they played by certain rules. They explained to him that they had tried to play without rules, but it was sheer pandemonium. No one won. No one wanted to play anymore. So they adopted these rules to make the game enjoyable for everyone.

What Piaget discovered was that they were playing marbles in exactly the same way they had as very young children in the first category, but there was an important difference. Now, the rules belonged to them! They had not been transplanted from another source. They were not their brother's rules or their older friend's rules. They believed this way of playing marbles had been invented by them.

This insight is useful for us in looking at faith development. As William James said, it's an important part of the process to lose your faith in order to rediscover a more realistic, more genuine kind of "twice-born" faith. Lostness, questioning, doubting—this is the stuff of a search for real faith, a faith that we can own, rather than have dumped on us by others. And like the bone that breaks and heals stronger at the broken place, it is a stronger faith than it was before because it has learned it can survive the loss of faith. Faith that can survive the loss of faith!

We need to die to all those old simplistic formulas. We need a "conversion" experience that won't allow us to believe that chanting slogans on Sundays will do the trick. We need a twice-born faith that takes on the calamities of life and doesn't deny them, but can still be faith in spite of them.

When we lose our childish faith and push through the lostness into something richer and more robust, we have eyes that have been opened to the reality of this life. We find a faith that is life-affirming, not life-denying. Our Sunday gatherings would then be opportunities to workshop on reality, to bring our doubts and questions and our pain and struggles, and then to work on developing a faith that can be sustained in the face of these things.

Once-born faith is needy. It requires simplistic solutions. The once-born soul needs success in relationships and business and health to affirm that he or she is okay, worthy of blessing. For that reason once-born souls use others to assure themselves success. If I'm successful, they say, then I must be okay! But the twice-born know that their dignity rests not on anything so insubstantial but entirely on the favor of God as revealed in Christ.

We know we are okay, precisely because the Creator of heaven and earth was crushed on the cross to reveal his grace and favor to us. If I'm okay, it's because God thinks so and not for any other reason.

When reborn in this way, we realize that our reliance on others to meet our every need, answer our every question, and ease our every pain is cloying and pathetic. We develop a robust and edgy faith that can cope with uncertainty and disappointment, which prefers to meet with others rather than use them. (Martin Buber once said, "Life *is* meeting.")

This twice-born faith can deal with gray areas, with paradox and loose ends. It questions everything and refuses to accept the easy answers. It is possible to have such a faith. It is a faith based on the person and teaching and work of Jesus, which embraces creation and incarnation. Such a faith frees us from always taking from others, because we know our personal dignity and worth is assured for us in Christ and, as the Apostle Paul declared, that in itself is good enough for us.

With eyes wide open

For too many Christians, God's grace in Christ is not enough. They tear around the place trying desperately to find other ways to help them believe that he really accepts them. When we've been touched by God's unrelenting love and re-born by God's pure grace revealed to us in Christ, our eyes are opened. We have come to attention. We see the hand of God all around us and we're committed to seeing the kingdom of God come in both ordinary and spectacular ways.

Psalm 30 is a psalm of David, written after a serious illness that threatened to take his life. Prior to contracting the condition, King David believed that God's hand was upon him and that this was evidenced in the many blessings that had befallen him since his youth. He was a distinctly once-born kind of soul, a man who seemed to need success to assure him of God's grace.

But as he lay dying, his faith was shattered. God was no longer playing by the rules. Through this experience of lostness, he discovered God's grace can touch us even in the midst of pain and uncertainty. Listen to the testimony of a twice-born soul, a man with eyes wide open:

> I will exalt you, O LORD,
>   for you lifted me out of the depths
>   and did not let my enemies gloat over me.
> O LORD my God, I called to you for help
>   and you healed me.
> O LORD you brought me up from the grave;
>   you spared me from going down into the pit.

Sing to the LORD, you saints of his;
    praise his holy name.
For his anger lasts only a moment,
    but his favor lasts a lifetime;
weeping may remain for a night,
    but rejoicing comes in the morning.

When I felt secure, I said,
    "I will never be shaken."
O LORD, when you favored me,
    you made my mountain stand firm;
but when you hid your face,
    I was dismayed. (vv. 1–7; NIV)

Here, David enters into lostness. He thought in his once-born phase that he would always be secure, forever blessed by a God who played by the rules. But when he came close to death, he wondered where God had gone.

Suddenly, the simplistic formulas didn't do the trick. In his desperation and doubt, he cries out:

What gain is there in my destruction,
    in my going down into the pit?
Will the dust praise you?
    Will it proclaim your faithfulness?
Hear O LORD, and be merciful to me;
    O LORD, be my help. (vv. 9–10; NIV)

Full of questions and despair he cries out for his life—and remarkably God meets him. David pushes through his faithlessness and searches for a faith that makes sense of suffering rather than denying it. Then, God opens his eyes:

> You turned my wailing into dancing;
>> you removed my sackcloth and
>>> clothed me with joy,
> that my heart might sing to you and not be silent.
>> O LORD my God, I will give you thanks
>>> forever. (vv. 11–12; NIV)

By losing his desperate, needy faith, he rediscovers a faith that resonates with gratitude—not because he worships a God who straightens and smooths every path, but because he knows one who empowers him to walk the rocky, winding roads as well.

The truly converted souls know that gratitude is the stuff of life. Our eyes are wide open because we've learned to see God's goodness in the most mundane things. We see God's grace revealed in movies, books, stories, good food and drink, sport and hobbies, cooking, small talk, raising kids, shared laughter, and strong coffee. And for this we are eternally grateful. Such gratitude sets us free from using others as objects. It liberates us from codependent, needy relationships.

If your eyes are wide open you'll know, as David eventually discovered, that the task of the living person is to praise God.

Chapter 7

Embracing Astonishment as a Spiritual Discipline

IN A PREVIOUS CHAPTER, WE SAW HOW ALL human beings yearn for experiences of awe and wonder, and how natural beauty puts us in our place as it snaps our breath away. But if we are to see God in the ordinary, we must do more than simply be open to encountering God in the crashing of the sea or the roar of thunder. We must develop the skill of being in awe of all expressions of truth and of beauty. This includes the interaction between peoples, the drama of stories, and the confluence of events; but also more.

Recovering the capacity for wonder

Hanging on a wall in my office I have a large reproduction of Vincent Van Gogh's *Vase with Twelve
Sunflowers* (1888). I also have several smaller copies
clipped from magazines or on postcards pinned on
noticeboards around the room. One of my daughters painted her own reproduction at school, and it
is proudly displayed as well. This image is something of an icon for me. Vincent painted around a
dozen versions of the same vase of sunflowers as a
kind of housewarming gift to Paul Gauguin, after
convincing him to come and board with him in
the Yellow House in the south of France. Huge,
dramatic, and breathtaking paintings, their brushstrokes are laid on so thickly and with such an
obvious sense of passion, I've often wondered
whether Gauguin worried about what he'd got
himself into when on arrival he was first confronted by such an obsessive act of welcoming
love.

Vincent's biographer, David Sweetman, put it
this way:

> He had, of course, painted sunflowers in Paris,
> but never the twisting, sun-searching southern
> blossoms he now depicted. They scream yel-
> low. Some are set in a yellow vase on a yellow
> table; some are violently alive, burning with

sunshine; others are dead, limp, exhausted, but not with the tranquil death of a real sunflower when it passes into a dry-brown state before scattering its polished seeds. This was death by self-immolation, a yellow suicide.[1]

Obsessive love! That's it. So overwhelmed was Vincent by Gauguin's acceptance of his invitation to Arles that he filled nearly every wall of the dingy little house he'd rented with massive canvasses vibrating with phosphorescent yellows and oranges and dramatic shades of green. I can't look—particularly at my original-sized reproduction replete with shadows underneath the generously ladled brushstrokes—and not reflect on the love that drove this wonderful man to such an act of hospitality.

The use of such brilliant color and violent impasto was initially repugnant to Gauguin (though in later life, when Vincent's star had risen, he claimed to have been impressed all along) and, six months after it began, their friendship ended abruptly with Vincent's most dramatic breakdown.

Why is this image so important to me? First, there's my knowledge of the story behind the image. I know about their creation and the intensity of emotion exhibited by their creator. They are an extravagant, obsessive, costly act of love—one that was rejected by their original recipient.

Such a dramatic display of affection is difficult for many of us to fathom, but surely this is exactly what the cross of Christ is about. It is God's extravagant love dished out in thick, hearty brushstrokes for all to see. And many of us, like the self-absorbed Paul Gauguin, are intimidated by such expressions of love. Vincent's sunflowers remind me of God's love for me and cause me to wonder at such love.

But second, they are visually enthralling in their own right. Visitors to my office are drawn to my picture, even though it's only a print. Some who aren't familiar with Postimpressionism or Vincent's work generally, ask me whether it's an original, because its quality is so excellent. Of course, I laugh; the original last sold for $58 million and will probably never sell again. They lean over a bookcase I have underneath the picture and allow their eyes to follow the contours of the heavy strokes. They are attracted to it. Even as a framed poster, it is magnetic.

Well, for some people it is. Those are the ones with the capacity for wonder. Some people have developed such a capacity, they have opened their eyes, they are attracted to beauty, and they can imagine the depth of the beauty of God when, in so fallen and polluted a world, something as wondrous as Vincent's sunflowers or Monet's lilies or music by Mozart or Van Morrison can be found.

This is no mean feat. The ability to slow down psychologically and spiritually (not to mention physically) long enough to come to attention to what is really happening around us is a discipline many people appear unprepared to embrace. To be aware, truly aware, to be astonished by the ordinary, is a noble and godly cause.

G. K. Chesterton is noted for having said that our perennial spiritual and psychological task "is to learn to look at things familiar until they become unfamiliar again."

Jesus himself is a man who seems astonished by the ordinary. He regularly refers to the mundane and sees these things as indicators of a wider truth. He spots lilies in a field, and they remind him of God's care for the human race. For him, the innocence of a child's eyes is an indicator of the true humility and awareness after which we all should strive. He makes references to mustard seeds, plowing, vineyards, and housework. He had an obvious capacity for wonder.

Being blocked to wonder

Why do so many of us find it so difficult to open our eyes? Why do we have such a hard time recovering our capacity for wonder? There are a few obvious answers.

First, we are rather too enamoured these days with the pragmatic disciplines. We're more interested in "getting things done" than in reflection and experience. For instance, we seem chiefly concerned with education for the sake of employment. In other words, we prefer training to education. We'd rather train an engineer or a scientist than educate a person to seek truth or beauty. People are expected to enter college with a clear goal in mind and to exclude all learning that doesn't equip him or her for the task at hand. We are goal-oriented, result-driven, outcome-obsessed.

The church has caught this cultural disease as well. Churches are more like corporations these days, as attuned to mission statements, goal-setting, and annual results as the rest of society. And inadvertently the church, in its drive toward "productivity," has also turned religious faith into a commodity. It seems we're just as concerned with training *ministers* as other educational institutions are with training engineers or doctors. As a result, skill-based, outcome-driven churches have become places for ordinary people to be *trained* in Christianity.

In some places, faith has contracted to be a purely intellectual exercise. To be taken by wonder, to be truly astonished by truth and beauty, is too slippery and uncontrolled a discipline for many current ministers to cope with.

Church has become a technical prospect in which the poets and the artists have been made to feel unwelcome. But perhaps the day will come when the more creative souls will be welcomed back. Walter Brueggemann, with whom we began this book, quotes American poet Walt Whitman in making this very point:

> After all the seas are cross'd (as they seem already cross'd),
> After the great captains and engineers have accomplish'd their work,
> After the noble inventors, after the scientists, the chemist, the geologist, ethnologist,
> Finally shall come the poet worthy of that name,
> The true son of God shall come singing his songs.[2]

I'm dreaming of that day as well!

Naturally, observing, appreciating, and being connected to God through our imaginations gets pushed aside in the interests of our task orientation. Some students who come into my office are so focused on getting an extension for a late assignment or so intent on seeking my advice on a particular issue that they probably don't even notice that, right behind me on the wall, there is a print measuring 1 by 1.3 meters of one of the world's great masterpieces. Some are so thoroughly concerned with completing their degree, achieving their study goals, that anything that gets in the way is scorned or put up with begrudgingly. Commitment to creating community or finding opportunities for reflection or solitude are rejected in the interests of getting the job done.

I've heard it put this way: if you had to meet a friend coming off a train at a crowded railway station, as you worked your way through the bustling commuters, you would be focused entirely on finding the face of your friend. You would be filtering out everything else that was going on, not observing in any detail the other faces or images around you. Your concern for finding your friend would limit your capacity to see anything else.

So it is generally. If we're focusing only on achieving our goals, we might very well achieve them—but at what cost! Surely, the Christian community is concerned with adopting a lifestyle that stands as a corrective to our modern world, not as a mirror of it. When ministers are as busy and as driven as CEOs of major companies, we have a problem.

Pragmatic, task-oriented people have great difficulty with what I'm saying. But as we noted earlier, you never get it if you don't slow down. I'm not wanting to appear naïve. There's nothing wrong with goals and objectives *per se*. The issue here is that we allow our obsession with our goals to block our capacity to be astonished by the wondrous.

The second block to being able to embrace wonder is self-absorption. As Canadian Catholic theologian Ronald Rolheiser says:

> Without making any moral judgements whatsoever, one can say that self-indulgence and excessive self-preoccupation are the antithesis of genuine awareness. When one is preoccupied with self and the needs of the self, these needs and preoccupations become a mirror through which one then perceives everything else.[3]

And as we saw in the previous chapter, whenever we see others only for their value in helping us meet our needs or their hindrance to our needs being met, we can never truly meet them or see Christ in them in any significant sense. Rolheiser refers to a mirror, but I see it more as a sieve, allowing through only that which fulfills me or comforts me or pleasures me. In this case, my openness to being discomforted, challenged, stretched, or disciplined is limited by my self-centeredness.

The self-absorbed personality is not taken by wonder, since wonder often unsettles us or intimidates us. Such a personality needs control. To be taken by beauty, to reflect on the daily displays of grace God sends our way, takes a capacity for abandon. We need to let go of our need to be in control and have our needs always met.

Recently, I visited Mengler's Hill above the beautiful Barossa Valley in South Australia. It had been raining constantly, and in the last hour of daylight the setting sun had finally burst through the heavy clouds, sending shafts of light in every direction across the valley floor, lighting up puddles, and turning the verdant fields and vines fluorescent. It was breathtaking. My companion sighed as I did, then said, "Imagine building a restaurant up here. You'd make a fortune."

It sounded like blasphemy. It was not enough to be moved by God making a pass at us in such a dramatic fashion. My friend had to think of a way of containing this scene, packaging it, making a profit out of it. Rolheiser says that in the non-contemplative personality, "there is a dramatic narrowing and distortion of awareness."[4]

And the third reason we often can't embrace wonder is our rigid, left-brain approach to accessing information. We need to process things through strict intellectual criteria. We are bound by the reason of technique and overly concerned with concreteness. Wonder invites us to an uncertain place, a place filled with mystery and experience but not necessarily with certainty and definition.

Again to Rolheiser who illustrates a similar point with the following example:

> Imagine someone coming up to you and telling you: "You know, I understand you. I've watched you grow up, I know your Myers Briggs results, I know your Enneagram number, and I am familiar with the dysfunctions of your family and your background. Besides that, you are French, and I know the temperament of the French! And you are so perfectly your mother's daughter! Oh yes, I do understand you!" Would you feel very understood?[5]

I think most of us would not only not feel understood, but quite the reverse. We would be offended by any attempt to define our personal complexity in so narrow a fashion. So Rolheiser continues:

> Compare that to someone who comes up to you and says: "You know, I don't understand you at all! You are one rich mystery! I've known you for twenty years and you still constantly surprise me!"[6]

This is a nonunderstanding that speaks of wonder and mystery, at complexity and depth. It implies respect and fascination, love and searching. To not be understood in this way is to have someone deeply understand us, our individual beauty and darkness.

The Bible speaks of God *knowing* every detail of both our anatomy and our personality, our motives and our longings. And yet it seems to me that this is always couched in a sense of wonder. It's as if God can't help but know all there is to know about us and God is still amazed by our complexity—not bored with it or unimpressed.

Well, it works in reverse, regarding our love for God. It always concerns me when preachers attempt to define, to explain, to prove God, to dissect God's nature, motives, and desires. God might know all about us and still be motivated by unending love.

But how much love can there be for God in those who dare to tell us what God thinks or feels at any given time! I can never get passed the great Martin Buber's maxim, "God is the Being . . . that may properly only be addressed, not expressed."

An instinct for astonishment

Have you ever been thoroughly moved by a piece of music, a painting, or a film and wondered where that instinctual reaction to something beautiful, creative, or richly complex comes from?

I recently received a letter from a friend in which he wrote the following:

Seeing God in the ordinary, as you say, has not always been the way of the church and I think that deep down I've always felt uncomfortable about this, although unable to identify what made me feel that way.

Some years ago I was moved to tears listening to some music (it was just music, not particularly Christian) and I remember wondering to myself why music existed. The only conclusion I could come to was that it is a gift of God to his people, Christian and non-Christian alike, and that we could see him in it even if it was written by a lascivious Mozart rather than a godly Wesley.

Now, that's an instinct for astonishment! "Deep down," he is saying, "I always felt uncomfortable about the prose-flattened, dry and dusty approach that church took to only seeing God in the so-called sacred realms." But it was music that took him to a sacred place not bounded by religious forms or formulas. We all have this instinct for astonishment if only we learn to listen to it, to sense the wondrous, and to explore God's grace in the myriad ways it comes to us.

I once met a fellow who felt that more creative honesty, more appreciation of beauty, more images of grace were apparent in his amateur theatre group than in his church. The artists of our society—actors, photographers, writers, painters, musicians—often feel both alienated from the church world and more impressed with the levels of community they find among themselves. This is a great shame, because artists have a great deal to offer us in teasing out our instinct for astonishment.

It has always occurred to me that most personality types fall into the following very broad categories: either we are builders, teachers, healers, or artists. And I mean this figuratively. Builders don't just operate on building sites. They can work in offices or schools. They're the ones who put things together, strategize, and plan. They build companies or curricula; they create products.

Teachers are the motivators of our world, the inspirers. They are purveyors of ideas and insight. Healers can be doctors and nurses, but they are also those who bring healing through compassion and care, through justice and discipline. Artists are those who point out beauty, who see the connections between things, who observe patterns and complementarities.

I think we're all a little of each, but I think we certainly favor one or two of them. I've known ministers who are definitely builders. They're motivated by production and outcomes. And there's nothing at all wrong with that. Other ministers are teachers. They inspire. After being taught by them we feel taken into realms beyond the ordinary. Yet again, others are healers. Their ministries have a distinctly therapeutic quality. Their words, their touch, their compassion bring growth and restoration.

And some others are artists. They use images and language in a way that makes our vision clearer. We see the beauty of connections because of their speech or their eye for the wondrous.

But it seems to me that our churches are dominated these days by builders and, to a lesser extent, teachers and healers. We're all trying to build a bigger church, create strategies, and develop objectives. We're meeting deadlines and fulfilling expectations. There's plenty of teaching, but it seems to be done by builders; it's technical, practical, and achievable. Even our healing is clinical and result-oriented. In this current climate when the country seems to have gone temporarily to the dogs, cats must learn to be circumspect, walk on fences, sleep in trees, and have faith that all the barking is not the last word. That, it seems, is where our artists have gone. They have the hardest time fitting in with this world of builders. Since builders can teach a bit and heal a bit, the teachers and healers feel reasonably at home (though never *really* at home), but artists just don't fit.

This isn't to denigrate the contribution of those whose chief calling is to build, but whenever any community gives itself entirely over to one discipline, it loses its center of gravity. One of the world's great artists, storyteller Garrison Keillor, put it this way:

> What keeps our faith cheerful is the extreme persistence of gentleness and humor. Gentleness is everywhere in daily life, a sign that faith rules through ordinary things: through cooking and small talk, through storytelling, through making love, fishing, tending animals and sweet corn and flowers, through sports, music and books, raising kids—all the places where the gravy soaks in and grace shines through.

I think artists like Keillor are often the first ones to spot these things. They see beauty in the ordinary things. They seem to have clearer perceptions of the delightful splendor all around us. The church must recover the opportunity for those who are artists—whether they call themselves so or are employed as such or not—to be heard, to make their distinctive contribution to the Christian community. The artistic mind is a healthy and necessary corrective that would infuse the teaching and healing of the church with a new depth and vitality. It is this very perspective that would assist

Christians to tap into their instinct for astonishment, to see God in the ordinary.

I cannot put it any better than another American writer with a capacity for wonder, the incomparable Annie Dillard:

> We are here to abet creation and to witness it, to notice each thing so each thing gets noticed. Together, we notice not only each mountain shadow and each stone on the beach, but we notice each other's beautiful face and complex nature so that creation need not play to an empty house.

> According to the second law of thermodynamics, things fall apart. Buckminster Fuller hinted at a reason we are here: by creating things, by thinking of new combinations, we counteract entropy so the universe comes out even. A shepherd looking at a mess of stars, thinking, "There's a hunter, a plough, a fish," is making mental connections that have as much real force as the very fires in those stars themselves.[7]

Only an artist could see life this way. As we emerge into another millennium, perhaps the time has indeed come for the poet, the true "son of God," to come singing his songs, to infuse our business-like church life with zest and interest, danger and uncertainty.

Unleashing our instincts

So, if we all share this basic instinct, how do we tease it out? How can we become more open to astonishment?

First, it takes courage and a commitment to hard work.

Remember the story of John Wesley's recovery of wonder, his renewed capacity to understand and experience God's grace? He wasn't prepared to give in to a heady, intellectual faith that offered no resistance to the haphazard nature of life. He kicked, screamed, and pushed at the edges of his faith until he could believe, really believe that God's grace was being revealed all around us—and especially in Christ's unending love for him.

Those of us who live in our heads, who have to assess everything through the eyes of logic and reason, who have made religious faith more a cognitive process than a spiritual one, need to embrace the courage it takes to let go of our need for control and open our eyes.

I don't mean to imply our reason is no longer helpful to us. Not at all! But we need to remember that it's *one* of our faculties to accessing information, not the only one. A recent movement in the church had as one of its major features the call for

Christians to stop thinking and just experience the Spirit of God.

I can understand someone calling for Christians to stop thinking so much that our single-minded devotion to logical, linear thinking blocks other pathways of learning. But there's no reason for us to completely abandon logic or rationality. Experience alone will be as dangerous as reason alone. The courageous will venture to balance both to some degree.

In the previous chapter, we looked at William James' advice on once-born and twice-born souls. The once-born soul requires rigid, fixed, logical structure to its worldview. It is not a courageous worldview. It is "designed," as it were, for those who prefer comfort and control. The twice-born soul can deal with uncertainty and doubt. He or she is not discomforted by mystery and searching. Such a faith worships God not because God and everything else in the world make sense, but because God empowers us to deal with a chaotic and uncertain world.

Next (and these are in no particular order), gratitude will open our eyes to wonder.

I'm becoming increasingly convinced that to truly embrace humanness we must learn the discipline of gratitude. Truly grateful people are generally fully alive to wonder. Have you ever noticed, when someone performs a particularly unexpected and selfless act on your behalf, how your gratitude toward that person reminds you of all the other ways he or she has been kind to you in the past? How many times, when you are feeling grateful to someone, do you hear yourself saying "She's *always* been there for me" or "Now that I think about it, he's a really great guy to me"? Your gratitude for the one act of kindness evokes memories of the full breadth of the person's love for you. I'm convinced that gratitude is one of the basic hallmarks of a spiritual person.

Those who are grateful for God's grace in Christ have their eyes opened to all the marvelous expressions of God's love around them all the time, both the welcome and the unwelcome ones. For love doesn't always show up in painless and agreeable ways. God's love can be expressed through difficult times of grief or failure, suffering or woe, but the grateful can see it for what it really is— God's attempts at helping us to grow.

A third important feature in recovering a capacity for wonder is humility.

The recognition that I am not the center of the universe, that I am deeply flawed and undeserving of God's love, puts me back in my place. In a very real sense, gratitude and humility are linked. The truly grateful are often equally truly humbled by the experience. They have a truer, fuller perspective. They are more connected with their place in the cosmos and see things more accurately.

Anyone who is a truly aware person must be humble. Humility is merely the result of accurate thinking. Therefore, rather than being some high-minded, holier-than-thou spiritual quality, humility as I understand it is a very down-to-earth trait.

Humility is about earthiness, reality, a true appreciation of our connectedness with a fallen world. The humble, since they are so doggedly realistic about themselves, have their eyes open to the realities that are going on around them.

The recapturing of innocence will go a long way to opening our eyes.

The Catholics call this revirginization, the return to a more naïve and innocent state. It means not that we forget all we know about the corruption and evils of this world, but that we work on developing ways to abandon cynicism and our jaded self-righteousness.

In my previous book, *Jesus the Fool*, I attempted to show how Jesus embodied a beautifully sublime, winsome naïveté. There's a lot of nonsense around these days about the purity and innocence of children. Personally, I don't find them all that innocent and I don't want to return to my childhood, but I know that Jesus commanded his

disciples to become like children if they were to in-
herit the kingdom. He referred specifically to the
humility of childhood. In adulthood, *we know too
much* for our own good.

The late Mother Teresa, though often accused
of playing the international media for her own
purposes (or the purposes of her order), was a case
in point. She had a wide-eyed innocence that expected the best, saw the best, believed the best.
When you have so childlike and guileless a faith,
you are more inclined to want to meet rather than
manipulate God (as if you could manipulate God).

Waking up is hard to do

In his autobiography, Greek writer Nikos Kazantzakis, the author of *Zorba the Greek* and *The Last
Temptation of Christ*, tells of an experience he had as
a young man going to visit a famous monk:

> Working up courage, I entered the cave and
> proceeded toward the voice. The ascetic was
> curled up on the ground. He had raised his
> head, and I was able in the half-light to make
> out his face as it gleamed in the depths of unut-
> terable beatitude. . . .
>
> I did not know what to say, where to begin. . . .
> Finally, I gathered up courage.

"Do you still wrestle with the devil, Father Makarios?" I asked him.

"Not any longer, my child. I have grown old now and he has grown old with me. He doesn't have the strength . . . I wrestle with God."

"With God!" I exclaimed in astonishment. "And you hope to win?"

"I hope to lose, my child. My bones remain with me still and they continue to resist."

"Yours is a hard life, Father. I too want to be saved. Is there no other way?"

"More agreeable?" asked the ascetic, smiling compassionately.

"More human, Father."

"One, only one."

"What is it?"

"Ascent. To climb a series of steps. From the full stomach to hunger, from the slaked throat to thirst, from joy to suffering. God sits at the summit of hunger, thirst and suffering; the devil sits at the summit of a comfortable life. Choose."

"I am still young. The world is nice. I have time to choose."

Reaching out with the five bones of his hand, the ascetic touched my knee and pushed me.

"Wake up, my child. Wake up *before death wakes you up."*[8]

"Wake up, my child." Now, there's good advice. But as Kazantzakis' anecdote reminds us, the call to come to attention requires courage and discipline, sacrifice and hard work. It cost Simone Weil her life, Vincent his sanity, and John Wesley his good reputation.

When I was a kid, there was a corny pop song that went, *breakin' up is hard to do.* Well, I'd like to change the words slightly and say that *wakin' up is hard to do.* It's not the easier way. Christ himself—the most awake person in history—taught us the importance of embracing sacrifice in order to find enlightenment. The truth is out there and it's found by those with their eyes wide open, but if you think that opening them is easy, think again. It takes truckloads of faith, but it's worth the price of admission.

Christ's death and resurrection was God's way of prying open the eyes of a sin-sick and world-weary human race. God offers truth freely. Some people say to me, "Oh, you're lucky. You have faith. I just can't believe. Once a person like me has these doubts, he or she cannot unthink them."

But I say that faith is not a matter of luck. It's a matter of being open to receive it. We are like new-born kittens, our eyes tightly shut, squinting in the harsh light of day. But if you dare to open wide your eyes of faith, you'll be surprised by what you see, by what it costs, and how it's worth it.

The existence of God, like the air we breathe, need not be proven. It is more a question of developing good lungs to meet it correctly. It takes exercise and big deep breaths. There's a simple prayer recorded in the Gospels that goes like this: Lord, I believe; help my unbelief.

You should try it sometime—if you haven't already.

Epilogue

Premeditation and the Hallowing of the Everyday

SINCE THE FIRST EDITION OF THIS BOOK WENT to print in Australia, I have often been asked how, as busy and productive people, we can really come to attention to see God in the everyday. Since I am also a busy person who enjoys having a high level of output in my life, some of my readers wonder how I do it. They want to embrace a contemplative lifestyle without having to join a monastic order. Many readers and many people who come to my seminars and workshops want to slow down, but they aren't prepared to slash too heavily into their schedules. "Can I slow down and come to attention and still keep my active lifestyle?" they ask.

My response is twofold: firstly, I encourage them not to rule out reorganizing their calendars. When I ask people to slow down, it doesn't always mean a big shift in their regular schedule, but it *may* in some cases. Some people just need to rearrange their lifestyles. This may mean cutting a few meetings, getting home a little earlier, taking a little longer over lunch. Slowing down, for some, might mean just that! Slowing down.

But my second response is to those of you who wish to remain active and productive, and even busy, but want to slow down while sitting in traffic or slow down while at your desk or while sitting in a class or at a meeting or taking children to school. It is possible. Seeing God in the ordinary is not only about how full or empty your calendar is, but about how attentive you're prepared to be even if rushing around.

I would like to introduce you to the spiritual discipline called *kavanah*. It is a Jewish term that roughly translates as premeditation, though it has a richer and deeper nuance than the English word usually conveys. The discipline of kavanah involves the preparedness for us to see that every action can be completed with an orientation toward God. The Jewish mystics and theologians like Martin Buber and Abraham Heschel embrace the discipline of kavanah as intrinsic to their seeing God in the ordinary.

Rather than seeing a separation between the world of thinking and the world of actions, the Jewish thinkers who embrace kavanah see that the one is an expression of the other, and vice versa. We are used to seeing the interior world of spirituality, reflection, prayer, and worship as somehow different from the exterior world of deeds and actions. To those who embrace kavanah, the true meaning of life is revealed in the deed. What matters is not what is being done, so much as the fact that every act is filled with sanctity—that is, with God-oriented intent. In other words, even the most profane, nonreligious activity can be given a God-oriented intent.

Martin Buber said,

> Enoch was a cobbler, and with every stitch of his awl that drew together the top and bottom of the leather, he joined God and the Shekinah (His glory) . . . man exerts influence on the eternal, and that is not done by any special works, but by the intention with which he does all his works. It is the teaching of the hallowing of the everyday.[1]

In order to understand kavanah, we must first understand this point: action is holy. That is not to say all aimless, ill-considered, thoughtless actions are holy. Rather, it is possible to live in a way that sacralizes ordinary actions. So that, like Enoch the cobbler, we can see the stitching of leather as a holy action. But Buber continues:

> The issue is not to attain to a new type of acting, which, owing to its object would be sacred or mystical; the issue is to do the one appointed task, the common, obvious tasks of daily life, according to their truth and according to their meaning. Also, one's works are shells; he who finishes his work rightly, hallowing it, encompasses the limitless in its core.[2]

So rather than having to engage in some overtly mystical or holy activity, we need to learn to value ordinary, unremarkable actions as potentially sacred. You don't have to join the monastery or go on a spiritual retreat to see God. God can be perceived in everyday activity. This is the first step in understanding kavanah; action is holy and we can understand something of God in our actions.

Another great Hebrew teacher, Abraham Joshua Heschel, put it this way: "Spiritual aspirations are doomed to failure when we try to cultivate deeds at the expense of thoughts, or thoughts at the expense of deeds. Is it the artist's inner vision or his wrestling with the stone that brings forth a sculpture? Right living is like a work of art, the product of both a vision and a wrestling with concrete situations."[3] This notion is not simply a Jewish one. It is also part of the heritage of the Christian experience. It can be found at the heart of the New Testament book of James, for example. James can't see how any distinction can be drawn between faith and works.

Unfortunately, this was an integration the Protestant Reformation nearly five hundred years ago couldn't embrace. In fact, Martin Luther reckoned that the book of James ought to be torn out of the New Testament. In his joy at the rediscovery of justification by faith, Luther oversteered the ship, emphasizing spiritual experience over holy action. The Protestant churches have belittled the holiness of action ever since. This is not essentially a Christian perspective. The Judeo-Christian worldview has always seen a complete integration between interior faith and exterior action.

As Heschel says, our lives are like a work of art: both the inner vision and the outward work are required to see it through to completion. There is a Jewish term for this holy action: *mitzvah*. When someone does a mitzvah with complete kavanah, he or she completes an act in such a way that his or her whole existence is gathered in it and directed in it toward God.

Kavanah, then, is the supreme form of premeditation. It is not about just doing things because you've been commanded to do them, but is about doing things with an awareness of the One who commands. It is the appreciation of being commanded, of the opportunity to do God's will. The goal is to find access to the sacred in the deed, any deed, and to partake of its inspiration.

We are used to hearing of the legal charge of *premeditated murder*, the taking of a life that involves planning and forethought by the perpetrator. Usually those found guilty of premeditated murder receive a harsher sentence than those guilty of manslaughter or of a crime of passion. The courts view the premeditation as having significant weight. A premeditated act is considered to be a more profound act than a thoughtless one.

Those who embrace kavanah have chosen to live a premeditated life! They are saying that they will live every action as a holy one and attempt with every deed to consider the Creator as being in it. Rabbi Heschel says, "The presence of God demands more than the presence of mind. Kavanah is direction to God and requires the redirection of the whole person. It is the act of bringing together the scattered forces of the self; the participation of heart and soul, not only of will and mind."[4] A premeditated life involves attentiveness, appreciation, and integration.

To premeditate your life is to choose to see a cobbler's labor (to take the example of Enoch again) as a commandment from God; to be attentive to God's voice in the labor itself; to appreciate the joy of creation and completion and the satisfaction of hard work; and to integrate both doing and thinking, both the sacred and the profane.

Think of it this way: when you're getting in your car to go to a meeting or the office or the workshop, don't think of the journey as a profane interlude between the holiness of home and work. Thank God for the opportunity to enjoy God's presence. See the car journey as a gift from God. As you turn the key in the ignition of the vehicle, pause; practice the presence of God. Premeditate what you're about to do. Try to access the sacred in the deed you're about to perform.

When you're in a football stadium watching a game, surrounded by thousands of fans, hotdogs, cheering, cups of Coke, stop. Premeditate what you're doing. Pause; look at your son. See the sacred in the act of sharing a day with him. Take your eyes off the game on the field and observe the faces in the crowd. Be attentive to God's presence. God is there, you know. But God is also present in your actions. Put your hand on your boy's head. Premeditate the action. Practice attentiveness, appreciation, integration.

Try it as you take the trash out. Try it when you take up a pen to write. In our home we have taken to lighting our living room with candles instead of using only electric lights. Of course, lighting a candle does have a religious connotation in the Christian experience. But when I light the thick yellow beeswax candles on our wrought-iron candelabra, I stop and watch the newness of the flame lick the dark air. I feel the gentle heat and look at the melted wax clinging to the iron stand. I'm attentive to God's presence. I'm appreciative of God's love and all the blessings I have experienced from those who share the light from these candles. I'm profoundly thankful. It has become a sacred act, every night. As Martin Buber says,

> Whether a deed will peter out in the court-yard, in the realm of things, or whether it will penetrate into the Holy of Holies is determined not by its content but by the power of decision which brought it about, and by the sanctity of intent which dwells in it. Any deed, even one numbered among the most profane, is holy when it is performed in holiness, in unconditionality.[5]

Now that's seeing God in the ordinary.

Endnotes

Chapter 1

1. Walter Brueggemann, *Finally Comes the Poet* (Minneapolis: Fortress, 1989), 1–2.

2. Ibid., 2.

3. Ibid., 3.

4. Ibid.

5. H. Richard Niebuhr, *Christ and Culture* (London: Nisbet, 1942).

6. Michael Frost, *Jesus the Fool* (Sydney: Albatross, 1994).

7. Millard J. Erickson, *Christian Theology* (Grand Rapids: Baker, 1992), 1041.

8. Luke 10:8–9; RSV.

9. 1 John 4:16b; NIV.

Chapter 2

1. Simone Weil, *Gravity and Grace* (London: Routledge & Kegan Paul, 1972).

2. Bob Dylan, "Every Grain of Sand" from the album *Shot of Love.*

3. Elie Wiesel, *All Rivers Run to the Sea* (London: Harper Collins, 1996), 164.

4. Martha Duffy and Richard Schickel, "Kubrick's Greatest Gamble," *Time* (15 December 1975): 72.

5. Matthew 13:14–15; NIV.

6. Matthew 7:7–8; NIV.

7. Chris Harding, unpublished policy document, Youth for Christ Australia.

8. Michael Frost, *Longing for Love* (Sydney: Albatross, 1996).

9. G. K. Chesterton, in Martin Wroe, *God: What the Critics Say* (London: Spire, 1992), 58.

10. John Wesley, *The Journal of John Wesley* (Chicago: Moody, 1974), 53.

11. Ibid., 64.

Chapter 3

1. Nicky Chiswell, "Copernicus" from the album *Copernicus.*

2. Harold Kushner, *Who Needs God* (London: Simon & Schuster, 1990), 52–53.

3. Psalm 8:3–4; my paraphrase.

4. C. S. Lewis, quoted in Philip Yancey, "Neat! Way Cool! Awesome!" *Christianity Today* (7 April 1997): 72.

Chapter 4

1. Robert Bly, *Iron John* (Reading, Mass.: Addison-Wesley, 1990), x–xi.

2. George Miller, "The Apocalypse and the Pig," in *The Sydney Papers* (Sydney: The Sydney Institute, 1996), 40.

3. Quoted in Ken Gire, *Windows of the Soul: Experiencing God in New Ways* (Grand Rapids: Zondervan, 1996), 80.

4. John Warwick Montgomery, ed., *Myth, Allegory and Gospel* (Minneapolis: Bethany, 1974), 21.

5. Ibid.

6. Ibid., 22.

7. George Miller, quoted in Janet Hawley, "The Hero's Journey," *Good Weekend Supplement, Sydney Morning Herald,* 14 October 1995, 57.

8. Stanley Hauerwas, *A Community of Character: Toward a Constructive Christian Social Ethic* (South Bend, Ind.: University of Notre Dame Press, 1981).

9. Scott Cowdell, "The Postmodern Church," *St. Mark's Review* (Summer, 1997): 14–20.

10. Ibid., 17.

11. Ibid., 18.

12. Ibid.

Chapter 5

1. Abraham Joshua Heschel, *God in Search of Man: A Philosophy of Judaism* (New York: Noonday, 1990), 202.

2. Ibid.

3. Ibid., 209.

4. Ibid., 210.

5. Carl Gustav Jung, in Joseph Campbell, ed., *The Portable Jung* (New York: Viking, 1971), 511–12.

6. David Tacey, "Sacred Canopy Offers No Shelter," *The Melbourne Age*, 22 July 1996.

Chapter 6

1. E. Stanley Jones, *Christ of the Indian Road* (London: Hodder & Stoughton, 1926), 100–101.

2. Quoted in M. Scott Peck, *A World Waiting to Be Born* (New York: Bantam, 1993), 3.

Chapter 7

1. David Sweetman, *The Love of Many Things: A Life of Vincent van Gogh* (London: Hodder & Stoughton, 1990), 277.

2. Walt Whitman, "Leaves of Grass," from Brueggeman, *Finally Comes the Poet*, viii.

3. Ronald Rolheiser, *The Shattered Lantern* (London: Hodder & Stoughton, 1994), 84.

4. Ibid.

5. Ibid., 86.

6. Ibid.

7. Annie Dillard, "The Meaning of Life," *Life* magazine, n.d.

8. Nikos Kazantzakis, *Report to Greco* (New York: Simon & Schuster, 1965), 222–23.

Epilogue

1. M. Buber, *Mamre* (Melbourne: Melbourne University Press, 1946), 78.

2. Ibid.

3. Heschel, *God in Search of Man*, 305.

4. Ibid., 316.

5. M. Buber, *On Judaism* (ed. Nahum Glatzer; New York: Schocken, 1968), 48.